UNBREAKABLE YOU

UNBREAKABLE YOU

CREATE, REVISE, REPAIR YOUR LIFE

JON DEAM, MD

COPYRIGHT © 2025 JON DEAM, MD
All rights reserved.

UNBREAKABLE YOU
Create, Revise, Repair Your Life

FIRST EDITION

ISBN   978-1-5445-4614-8 *Hardcover*
           978-1-5445-4616-2 *Paperback*
           978-1-5445-4615-5 *Ebook*

To my grandfather, John Deam, MD, and to all those who keep on keeping on.

CONTENTS

INTRODUCTION..11

PART 1: LIFE IS ITERATIVE
1. YOU DON'T START WITH THE STATUE; YOU START WITH THE MARBLE............21
2. DON'T GET INTO A CAGE WITH A TIGER YOU DON'T KNOW..........................27
3. DON'T BE A SPECTATOR IN YOUR OWN LIFE...31
4. YOU'RE NOT STEPPING INTO THE FINAL CHAPTER, JUST THE NEXT ONE........37

PART 2: LETTING GO
5. YOU CAN'T SOLVE THE EQUATION WHEN YOU'RE ONE OF THE NUMBERS........47
6. THE TRUTH CAN HURT BUT NOT FACING IT CAN SCAR 51
7. SOMETIMES IT'S NOT GIVING UP, IT'S LETTING GO 55

PART 3: BEING GOOD ENOUGH
8. A.I.G.E. SYNDROME 61
9. YOU'RE NOT THE SUM OF YOUR MISTAKES 67
10. EVERYONE HURTS; NO ONE IS BROKEN 73

PART 4: MAKING CONNECTION

11. THE HARDEST ROAD IS THE ONE YOU TRAVEL ALONE 83
12. INTIMACY ISN'T BUILDING YOUR CASTLE WALLS NEXT TO EACH OTHER; IT'S OPENING THE GATES 89
13. YOU CAN'T EXPECT OTHERS TO FEEL BETTER ABOUT YOU THAN YOU FEEL ABOUT YOU 97

PART 5: DON'T WAIT FOR TOMORROW

14. CHANGE IS UNDEFEATED 105
15. CHANGE NOW OR NOW WILL CHANGE YOU 109
16. IF YOU PLAY DEAD TOO LONG, THE BEAR WILL EAT YOU ANYWAY 115

PART 6: BUILDING RESILIENCE

17. RESILIENCE ISN'T SHOWING UP WHEN IT'S ALL GREEN LIGHTS; IT'S SHOWING UP DESPITE A LOT OF RED ONES 123
18. RESILIENCE ISN'T MEASURED DAY TO DAY 129
19. BECOMING UNBREAKABLE 133

CONCLUSION 139
ACKNOWLEDGMENTS 143
ABOUT THE AUTHOR 145

DISCLAIMER

Although I am a doctor, I am not your doctor. This book is not medical advice and is not intended as a substitute for the medical advice of physicians. The reader should regularly consult a physician in matters relating to their health, particularly with respect to any symptoms that may require diagnosis or medical attention. No material in this book is intended to be a substitute for professional medical advice, diagnosis or treatment. Never disregard professional medical advice or delay seeking treatment based on something you have read in this book.

INTRODUCTION

HOW DO BABIES START BREATHING?

Very suddenly, it turns out.

Those first big breaths are magic—one of the coolest events I saw during medical school. Sallow gray and blue flash instantly to a lively pink or rich brown. The change is instantaneous and seems miraculous. The baby goes from something that looks alien to something that looks like us, that looks perfect, all in a moment.

Then the doctors, nasal cannula nearby to provide supplemental oxygen just in case, slap the baby's butt or tickle its feet. There's usually a second of silence where everyone, including the baby, is holding their breath. Then the little mouth opens and gulps its first air.

When fetuses are in the womb, they get less oxygen than they do in the open air. The mother breathes for the fetus, transferring oxygen through the umbilical cord, but she uses a lot of that oxygen, too. The deoxygenated blood makes a seconds-old baby's skin gray and lips blue, something we can't see until the moment of birth, when, for an instant, the new baby is still connected to its maternal lifeline.

For those who've had the privilege to see it, a healthy baby being born may be the only moment in life that is perfect.

But the moment one life stage moves to another doesn't normally happen this quickly. This perfectly. Perceptions of perfection are always subjective. For babies, that first dramatic, perfect breath is a moment of bewilderment and chilly discomfort. They don't know their first breath is one of billions. The first thing they do with their newfound lungs is cry as hard as they can.

Jarring experience is necessary for living. But as adults we tend to expect everything to be perfect. We expect ourselves to be perfect, and our identity as a perfect person comes to rest on singular decisions.

Should I have a baby?
Should I go to medical school?
Should I go on this first date?
Should I get married?
Divorced?
Sell my business?

All these questions lead to one: am I doing life right?

For many, these questions come at a common life inflection point. A crossroads A decision you feel is important to your future happiness, health, and success—and so you struggle to get to the other side of it. You get stuck because the decision feels black and white. Everything feels like it is riding on this decision, which means it has to be perfect. The anxiety over making the right decision, choosing the right path, is crushing.

And it's making you very, very unhappy.

What's more, this inability to move forward seems to be tainting everything else in your personal and professional life, leading to the usual suspects of unhappiness: stress, anxiety, anger, ill health, and dysfunctional coping mechanisms like confrontation, avoidance, isolation, drugs, and alcohol.

You don't like who you are now. But you're not sure of who you should or could be.

The discord between your real and ideal life creates feelings of doubt. You are so uncertain of what comes next, what path you should take, that you get stuck at the crossroads, unable to take the next step.

No choice is so grand that it belongs on a pedestal. One decision rarely makes or breaks a life. Most are pretty mundane. The truth is, you can go back to a decision later. Get more life experience, or relationship advice, or mentorship and do something about it. There are plenty of people I've known who don't go straight through from a bachelor's degree to a doctorate. Who have more than one marriage. Who've created and sold multiple businesses, or who became mentors or community leaders after handing off their companies.

Your vision of who you are now and who you think you're supposed to be isn't necessarily the right one. It might not be working to bring you the success and happiness you hope for. Because sometimes, this vision is rooted in misconceptions of who you are, what you want, or what others are expecting of you.

Why does doing life right—and all the books telling you how to do so—feel so complicated and abstract?

Why do you feel so stuck?

HOW I CAME TO WRITE THIS BOOK

When I first started thinking about writing this book, I attended an authors' workshopping event, curious to know what to expect when a book comes together. I sat quietly in the audience absorbing everything. As a psychiatrist, I'm used to listening.

One of the authors in the group who'd had some success called me out, "You haven't shared anything," she said. "What kind of book would you write?"

With a few more probing questions, she had me talking about the basic life wisdom I'd gathered from almost two decades in the fields of medicine and mental health. By this point, I'd had thousands and thousands of conversations with people from all walks of life, from those experiencing homelessness and drug addiction to high-powered CEOs to Hollywood entertainers to twenty-something young women who'd never been on a date. And over all these conversations there was a small collection of themes that kept showing up over and over again. Themes that contributed to feelings of not being good enough. To feeling stuck. To feeling broken. Themes that appeared to be universal across all client populations, which made sense, since all humans go through the same life stages from birth to death. Themes that everyone, including myself, had to accept if we wanted to live happy, healthy, and whole lives.

- Life is iterative.
- Holding on means letting go.
- Being good enough starts with you.
- Connections carry you through.
- Don't wait for tomorrow or you may miss it.
- Resilience is built one step at a time.

After sharing these themes, the author looked at me in silence for a moment, then she asked, "Why are you holding this information hostage? Aren't there people out there, who are not your clients, who could benefit from this wisdom too?"

Honestly, I didn't have a good answer for her.

Her question was a catalyst. It helped me confront my own fears that blocked me from writing. Why *didn't* I write down my knowledge and share it?

Many of the popular books on self-help and life coaching come from two camps. The first camp is full of facts and figures from professional medical providers and tends to sound like a textbook. The second camp may also contain research couched within a more conversational tone, but the authors are not credentialed medical or mental health professionals. As someone who's seen babies born and people die—who's experienced firsthand the big moments universal to all human life and the uncertainties and gray areas that come with it—I wanted to bridge the gap and bring everyday readers a relatable and easy-to-read self-help guide from a real doctor and psychiatrist.

I also knew my brand of therapy attracted people who avoided the usual talk therapy approach. Traditional therapy is great for looking backward. We need to know where we came from. This family system, that education, those traumas, the patterns that sometimes work for us but often don't—all contribute to where we are now. But staying in the past doesn't always provide a path to the future. My specialties of positive psychology and life coaching focus on looking forward. Where are you now? What are the things you need to learn? And what are the steps to get to this version of you that you want to be? Is that version actually the one that you should be? If moving forward means revisiting the past, so be it, but that's not where we start.

I'd spent most of my professional life taking complicated medical concepts and experiential knowledge and turning them into bite-size one-liners for my clients. So why not share these truisms with the wider audience of a book? Why couldn't people far distant from me also get these truisms, which might be the catalyst to help them confront the fears that blocked them from living a fulfilling life and reaching their goals?

So, I set out to write down what I know about becoming unbreakable.

WHAT'S IN THIS BOOK, AND WHAT ISN'T

As a medical professional, I have to insert the normal disclaimer. I'm a doctor, but I'm not *your* doctor. This is a book, not a doctor's office. It does not substitute for medical care or therapeutic work. It can't diagnose a mental health condition. It can't prescribe medication. And there's no guarantee the advice found within these pages will heal you. This is for educational and illustrative purposes only, a nudge to get you going. If any of the stories I use resonate, I encourage you to seek out a professional who can tailor a treatment plan to your unique needs and situation and support you through the many decisions and journeys you make moving forward.

While I use real client stories in this book as illustrations and examples, the characters of the clients themselves are works of fiction. They are composite characters, combining backgrounds and details of multiple case histories into representative examples of the common types of clients I encounter. The names of these characters, of course, are all made up, and are not intended to call out any real person who might read this book. And just to make sure of their fictional nature, you may recognize some names from popular movies and books.

Because these characterizations of clients trend toward the general, as does the advice, there are some complexities of life that are lost. The positive, simple words here are not intended to discount or make light of the very real and hard struggles of those negotiating complex trauma or mental illness. One book cannot disentangle a person's past, which is why I state again, the advice here only shows you what you might need to work on. From here, you can find an expert who can support you doing the work.

I want the experience of reading this book to be as close to a one-on-one conversation with me as I can get in this format. Unlike other books in this genre, I chose to steer away from citing stats and studies. I don't quote the medical journals or psychological theories that underpin my methods to my clients, so I'm not going to do so to my readers, either. Instead, I'll reference what I always reference to coach someone through their problems: a collection of short sayings, personal stories, thought experiments, and pop culture analogies.

The arrangement of this book presented a bit of a challenge. I personally hate long chapters, and the short sayings lent themselves to a shorter format. There are six parts, divided roughly into the six themes listed above. These six main themes build on each other—it's easiest to understand the second theme if you understand the first and so on. The part order is not intended to proscribe specific steps that must be done in a particular order. The themes are interconnected and overlap. Each main theme has several small chapters headed by related truisms and metaphors that go with it. Hopefully, you'll find yourself going back to these truisms every time you need them because, let's face it, no real path forward is easy or straight or free of side quests.

To sum up, this book is a compilation of my greatest hits, the bits of advice that resonate most. But it's not meant to be a life hack, or a quick fix. Working to change ingrained mental, emotional, and behavioral patterns takes time. It's like going to a gym to build a strong body. You can't just drop twenty pounds overnight; you have to work at it, and that work can spill into many of the connected parts of your life.

To get unstuck, to build the mental strength and resilience that make you unbreakable, takes hard, sometimes painful, actions. It takes making healthy choices consistently over time, forming a new ritual for living. Maybe the principles outlined here will prompt you to make a different choice than you did yesterday. Maybe it won't. Maybe it will plant a seed that only flowers months or years from now.

Will this book answer that all-important question, "Am I doing life right?" No. It won't. Because that's the wrong question.

The real question should be: "Why do I think there is a right way to do life?"

The wisdom in this book can help you move through the old traumas and narratives that block you from positive growth. You'll have more confidence and trust that taking any direction is better than taking no direction. And you'll have the mindset to not beat yourself up if you encounter bumps along the way.

I can't tell you for sure how your journey will end. I can't tell you what path to create. That's not how coaching works. This book won't end your journey, but it can give you the self-trust to start it.

It *is* possible to ditch the old fantasy narratives and write another. One that's more workable. More real. More adaptable. More resilient. And more reflective of what actually happens when people go about doing the hard task of living.

So let's crack open those old assumptions you have about yourself so you can get on a new, more centered, more fulfilling path. One that allows you to Create, Revise, Repair your life and become an unbreakable you.

PART 1

LIFE IS ITERATIVE

CHAPTER 1

YOU DON'T START WITH THE STATUE; YOU START WITH THE MARBLE

I'D BE WILLING TO BET THAT WHEN MICHELANGELO SET OUT to carve the statue *David*, he didn't know exactly how it would look. He may have had an idea based on many sketches or models, but looking at that big hunk of white marble must have been slightly intimidating because the huge block of solid white marble the church fathers had chosen for the commission was flawed. He knew he'd have to work around those flaws if he was going to bring his creation to life.

You don't start with the statue; you start with the marble. The sculptor slowly chips away at a big block of rock until a rough shape emerges, then chips away a little more every day, carefully and slowly so as not to break off too much, until that shape gets to something worth admiring. Michelangelo took three years to complete his own masterpiece.

YOU DON'T START WITH THE GOAL; YOU START WITH THE DECISION.

The raw material that has the potential to be something beautiful.

People think they have to get it right the first time and the life decisions they make fall to either side of a knife's edge—good or bad, right or wrong, perfect or imperfect. More experienced sculptors thought the marble for the *David* was bad, destined for failure. So they refused to go forward with the project, leaving it to a twenty-six-year-old upstart who then created an iconic piece of art because he trusted he could work around the stone's flaws.

So how many imperfect stones have you been given? And how many have you refused to carve because you were too afraid to get it wrong?

Success is not about making the most perfect decision. It's about making the one that feels right for right now and having some faith that you'll figure out how to work around any flaws that crop up. We often don't even know what's a good or bad decision until we're well into it. And we definitely don't know how others perceive what we do.

David was supposed to be one of a set of sixteen statues, hidden up near the roof of the Duomo where no one would see the details. Background art for the worshippers. But when Michelangelo was done and the statue was delivered, the church fathers were so impressed with it they couldn't bear to stick it up on a wall somewhere. They thought it was too perfect. So they made a special spot and pedestal for it, and now art worshippers of all ages go to Florence just to see it.

What others think of your creations is not the same as what you think of them. Mostly, others judge what you do less harshly than you do. And we have no idea how these works will be perceived. Michelangelo took a B-grade project and made A-grade work. Because he liked the challenge of it.

Statues are iterative projects. Over time, a giant slab turns into a beautiful thing, one tiny revision, one miniscule repair, at a time. Any single strike of hammer to chisel isn't going to make a big difference in the whole scheme of things. If a hammer blow hits an unseen fault in the marble and the block cracks, there are more blocks of marble in the quarry. A broken statue is something every sculptor will face and the art that fills museums and private collections today comes from artists who didn't let imperfect materials or potential failure stop them.

Even when you think the statue is done, it could degrade and get dirty. It could get chipped. It could fall off its pedestal and break clean through. The *David* now has cracks in his ankles, and conversations are being had about how to stabilize him when and if it's needed.

Something as seemingly strong and permanent as stone still needs a constant regimen of maintenance to keep everything working and looking its best. The process of create, revise, repair isn't a one and done; it's cyclical. And that cycle doesn't go just one way. You can bounce back and forth among any stage of the process depending on what's needed.

Iterations or maintenance regimens are akin to personal rituals, to borrow an idea from Tony Robbins. Rituals are the habits and routines that make up day-to-day life. Some rituals are obvious, like a person with a gym routine. Some are not, like someone using tapping to help stave off a panic attack. Helping yourself is not a quick fix, a life hack, or a light switch. You're going to create, revise, repair for the rest of your life, and building these habits is a part of that process.

One caveat here: rituals also change with the phases of our lives. We all have regrets. "I wish I'd done that differently" will catch us once in a while as our brain replays something that resulted in hurt or embarrassment. But regrets are few and far between for many of us. Those who move smoothly through life are okay with where their paths led them, and the regrets they have, if any, don't weigh on them. When you're forty, you'll look back with regret on things you did when you were twenty that felt good at the time, and at sixty you'll look back on forty. Only further life experience actually makes those earlier experiences a regret. So why regret a mistake done out of ignorance?

Let go of the idea that you have to get it right all the time because, even if you think you're right right now, when you look back on that stage of life, you may think you got it wrong. So who's to say what "right" is when even our past and future selves don't agree?

LIFE IS ITERATIVE.

It's a constant process of create, revise, repair that never stops as long as the earth makes trips around the sun. So why keep worrying about this first step? Any step, really?

Clark had terrible health anxiety. He always worried that something was wrong with his heart, despite being young and healthy. We sat in my office and counted up how old he was. How many years? Months? Days? Hours? Minutes? How long has his heart been beating? An average heart rate is sixty beats per minute. That's once per second. There are sixty minutes in an hour, twenty-four hours in a day, three hundred and sixty-five days in a year. By the time you're thirty, your heart's beat nearly a billion times.

When you take a step back and look at how many times something repeats in life, it's a much bigger number than you think. And you've lived through those previous chances, so what are the actual chances this next one will be the big one? The fatal flaw?

You're going to be dealing with chances and choices for the rest of your life. It doesn't matter what stage of your life you get to that core question: am I doing life right? You're going to keep revisiting and revising your answer to that question anyway. You get lots of heartbeats. You get another turn about the sun. Things always cycle back through. This is just one phase or iteration of yourself.

Creation makes something. Anything. There is no perfection, or even greatness, in a first attempt. But a first attempt is just that. Not second. Not fourth. First. But a first attempt gives you a thing you can then revise until it gets to a point that feels right. If revising breaks the thing you created, or makes it worse, you can move on to repair, fixing the mistake or starting again fresh.

Does *David* look exactly the way Michelangelo first envisioned it? Did Michelangelo look at his finished statue and see a few flaws? At what point did Michelangelo let go of the preconceived notion that *David* was only supposed to be background art high on the Duomo's shelf and let his statue be a beautiful, revolutionary thing that millions have enjoyed for centuries? Does it even matter to us, who revere his work now, what he thought?

I'm willing to bet no sculptor's finished work came out exactly like their original vision. The end work isn't necessarily worse or better than the original model; it's its own thing. The artist knows this and lets the marble speak for itself.

At some point, you have to stop with the theory and act to figure it out for yourself. Start chiseling away at a block of marble you selected to start making what you think is the best thing for you at that moment, knowing the end result of creation looks different every time the hammer falls.

We don't remember the names of the people who quit when things looked hard. Who refused to go forward when the marble was cracked. We remember the names of people who kept going and tried.

The marble never had to be perfect to be beautiful. It had to meet an artist who saw beauty in it.

Life is big and bold and full of surprises and there's no right or wrong way to get there. Create, revise, repair. It's the first step to an unbreakable you.

CHAPTER 2

DON'T GET INTO A CAGE WITH A TIGER YOU DON'T KNOW

DON'T GET INTO A CAGE WITH A TIGER YOU DON'T KNOW seems like obvious advice to follow. But what if you *do* know the tiger?

Tigers living in zoos or variety shows have trainers who've worked with individual animals for years. They know the tiger's personality and behaviors. To a certain extent, the tiger trusts the trainer, and the trainer trusts that they can work safely with the big cat because of the bond they share. But this relationship doesn't exist for the rest of us. Getting into a cage with a potentially dangerous animal without knowing how to read and respond to that animal is an objectively bad decision. But for the tiger's regular trainer, getting into its cage is a calculated risk they are willing to take based on hours of personal experience and good results.

There are so many ways to manage a choice, and what makes a decision okay for you might not be okay for me because of my experience, knowledge, and the tigers I know. The absolute, life or death, put-your-hand-on-a-hot-burner-and-pull-away moments are actually fewer than you'd think. But for those who get chronically stuck, it feels like those right/wrong choices are everywhere.

Two oppositional choices form a binary. Both sides cannot occupy the same space at the same time. It's either perfect or imperfect. Win or lose. Succeed or fail. The other thing about binaries: one side is always positive and the other negative. No one wants to be on the bad side, except, maybe, Anakin Skywalker. So we either avoid choosing a side or prolong making the choice until our hand is forced one way or the other, often by factors beyond our control.

But when we think a decision is binary, with only a yes/no, absolutist outcome, we put ourselves in a frustrated, painful space inside our own minds. Each side of the binary cannot occupy the same space in this mindset. Right and wrong paths have to remain on either side of their line going in separate directions. Once one is chosen there is no going back, and we arrive at either a good or bad outcome. If we think everything rides on making the right, perfect decision, and leave no room for play and mistakes, then the thought of moving forward and making the wrong decision freezes our momentum. We can't move forward with anything until we know for sure which way to go.

Nature doesn't recognize right and wrong. No one tiger is good or bad. They just are. Each possesses a set of characteristics and experiences that make them more or less easy for a particular person to handle. So the decision to get into a cage with a tiger isn't a binary, either.

Each doer learns something valuable from each experience. No one attempt is good or bad. It just is. Life's a crayon box full of different colors, shades, and nuance. Why limit yourself to only two?

Life is not built on binaries: white or black, right or wrong, perfect or imperfect, normal or abnormal. Those are human inventions. Life is iterative, a constant cycle of creation, revision, and repair. There is no perfect choice, or perfect you, and certainly no perfect way to get into a cage with a tiger. Yet we invent that perfect self anyway and expect it to make all our perfect choices.

Now take a moment and let the idea that we compare ourselves to a perfect fantasy version of ourselves sink in. Do we do this with other fictional characters? Do we beat ourselves up because we are not as strong as Superman? As fast as the Flash? As smart as Batman? No. But we certainly get anxious when the superheroes we imagine we should be walk into the room.

No matter how perfect you are trying to be, life's going to throw a monkey wrench into the works. "It's a trap!" as Admiral Ackbar would say to the Rebel Fleet, flying toward a quiet Death Star. Every decision can lead to bad things. On your way to the zoo, deciding to take five extra minutes to pick up coffee may put you at that intersection at the exact moment someone runs a red light. No one can totally avoid risk no matter how much they know.

There are few objectively bad decisions. The amount of risk attached to a decision depends on the context of that decision—the frame of reference of the decision-maker. *You* might not want to get into any one cage with any one tiger at any one time.

Getting hung up on any one decision hangs us up. If we only focus on the risk of death, the negative side of a binary, we'd never take the chances that make us tiger tamers.

MAKING DECISIONS REQUIRES TAKING RISKS.

We have to pick up that chisel, found that company, get in that tiger cage. Otherwise, we are forever a spectator in our own lives.

CHAPTER 3

DON'T BE A SPECTATOR IN YOUR OWN LIFE

A SPECTATOR IS SOMEONE WHO STAYS IN THE STANDS AND watches the game. They have no control over the outcome in the field. Everything from their perspective is pure chance—injuries, foul plays, last- minute scores—no matter how much they care about the outcome.

But the game will go on whether they are on the field or not. The final score will be called whether they are watching or not.

**IF YOU LEAVE IT TO CHANCE,
YOU CHANCE IT TO LEAVE.**

If you are a spectator in your own life, you are letting chance—what happens to you versus what you do—take away your power to create, revise, and repair. You let chance drive the bus, directing where you should go and what you should do.

I met Barry during my residency. He was a veteran whose diagnoses were pretty typical of the adult population: anxiety and depression. He was functioning okay at his job, and his medications kept him stable. On paper, he looked like he was doing fine. But one day he came into a session and said something not so typical.

"I've never been on a date," he told me, his ears turning red. "I'm fifty years old and I've never had sex. I've never even had a kiss."

I dug further to find this one perception of failure held him frozen and had spread like a fungus to affect his other relationships. He couldn't talk to women because he dreaded the inevitable confession of his virginity. He wouldn't hang out with his coworkers. He didn't make friends. He was afraid people would ask him about his love life. He didn't want them to think he was abnormal. The sheer possibility of admitting to his singleness became a monster on a hill—a dread so big and powerful it overwhelmed and consumed his whole social life.

The monster on the hill takes its inspiration from Don Quixote, the elderly commoner who wants to be a knight and save the damsel in Cervantes's epic tale. Don Quixote, as a good knight, must fight monsters, which he creates out of everyday objects. In one of the book's most famous scenes, Don Quixote tilts his rusty lance at a windmill on a hill, thinking it's a dragon. In his imagination, Don Quixote made a monster out of a windmill in the distance, something he couldn't see clearly with his fading eyesight.

As we get closer to the monsters we only look at from a distance, we find out they're benign. Not a danger, just shadows on a wall. Nothing. The tilting at windmills metaphor resonates through the ages, as popular culture never grows tired of referencing it (including me).

Was the veteran's lack of romantic partners outside the common experience? Sure. Was it really that unusual? No, not really. But he'd built a whole dreadful story around it as he looked at it from a distance. His fear of dating had grown into a fear of perception. What would others think of him? Would they reject him for his behavior? Would he be considered a monster himself? The anxiety of these potential judgments made his social anxiety exponentially worse over time.

His monster kept him sidelined. He was a spectator in his own life when it came to personal relationships. He watched other people play the game and live their lives, and after decades of inaction, he woke to the fact that he didn't like being a spectator. He was watching life pass him by and was getting to the point where he thought it was too late to live a full life. The last lonely chapter of his life loomed in front of him, and it was then he realized he was more afraid of what his future would look like *without* action than what it would look like with it.

To get the things he wanted and needed, Barry would have to step onto the field, knowing not all his plays were going to work. No first date goes like the fairy tale, despite what the movies want us to believe, and that's true whether you start dating at fifteen or fifty.

To play, you have to get in the game. Good players may assess their moves before they make them, but they also assess them after the game. Could they do something differently next time to get better results?

First tries are crap. We have to acknowledge that truth and move on to the part where we can practice and get better. You have to decide you want the chance to win and then get in there. Cover yourself with mud, grass stains, and sweat. Scrape a knee. Twist an ankle. Hit a foul ball. Experience the messiness of it all. The game will kick your butt. You're not going to win every game you play, and that's okay. That's expected. There are lessons there, too.

As Teddy Roosevelt said, "The credit belongs to the man who is actually in the arena." The man who dares greatly has no regrets. Not so the man sitting on the sidelines afraid of failure, opting for a cold existence devoid of achievement and purpose. Roosevelt knew both winning and losing came with playing the game. He did both. It seems obvious and an acceptable trade-off for happiness.

So what keeps people rooted to their seats? The answer turns out to be simple: they think they must win every game. And they think some great personal imperfection will prevent them from winning. So they don't even try.

There are going to be moments in life that break you a little bit. Maybe a lot. Then you take a step back, see where the fault lines are, and work to fix them. At least, when you are fixing something, you are still playing the game. Still creating, revising, repairing.

LIFE ISN'T KEEPING SCORE.

Accomplishments aren't points that get added up at the end of your life so you can see if you've won. Life isn't a win-or-lose game. It's a game that keeps going until you die, and the only losers are those who don't play at all. Making mistakes doesn't mean you lose the whole game, just that you didn't succeed on that play. The game, and all its possibilities, is what matters; the scraped knees just show you had fun in the arena. Now you know better for next time and can revise your strategy.

Even mistakes that seem like losses at first can turn out to be wins. For medical students, the greatest example of this is the discovery of antibiotics. According to legend, one Friday in 1928 someone left a window open in Alexander Fleming's lab, allowing mold spores to contaminate samples of bacteria being grown in petri dishes. Fleming, who was growing the bacteria, saw the mold colonies when he came into the lab on Monday. He was about to scrap the whole project when he saw cleared rings around the spots of mold where the bacteria had died. Fleming realized the mold was producing some sort of chemical that was inhibiting bacterial growth. That chemical was named penicillin.

Fleming's serendipitous mistake would lead to one of the greatest advances in modern medicine, arguably one of the biggest turning points in human population growth and longevity as a whole swath of deadly diseases ceased to be an issue.

Outcomes are what outcomes are. To live, you have to do it, even if it's imperfect. Because it's imperfect. You can't go wrong if you start moving because you'll get somewhere different than where you were before. "One sometimes finds what one is not looking for," as Dr. Fleming famously said.

Life is an experiment. You won't even know if you made a good or bad decision until after you make it. If the results are good, you can rinse and repeat, maybe doing it even better this time. If results are bad, you can change how you do something next time.

Revising is a little like stopping to take your temperature. What's your health look like after all that? For example, maybe there's a job in front of you. You think you want a promotion. Maybe you have some trepidation about applying. Are you good enough? Do your skills match all the criteria? People talk themselves out of applying to jobs all the time with these types of questions.

If you apply, what's the worst that could happen to you? If you apply and get the job, same question. You don't like it? Then you can revise and repair by putting a finger on the pulse of what you now know you don't want so you can pivot and look for something that's a better fit. At least, you know not to look for that type of job again. And what if you love the job and it's the best thing you could have done? How could you know that until you're in the role and doing the tasks?

The same goes for other life decisions. After you make one, you can ask yourself, "Is that okay? Is that what I want it to be?" If it isn't (and it usually isn't in the early going), you can revise and repair.

No decision is perfect. No action comes without risk of failure. But doing lots of small imperfect things becomes greatness over time. That's the beauty of it. So expect imperfection and embrace it. You may save millions of lives.

Getting onto the field is the first step, but it's not the only step. There will be many actions, and many steps taken, throughout a life.

CHAPTER 4

YOU'RE NOT STEPPING INTO THE FINAL CHAPTER, JUST THE NEXT ONE

THERE'S AN OLD SAYING: "AN APPLE A DAY WILL KEEP THE doctor away." But what would that actually look like? Well, that would be 365 apples times seventy-six, the average life expectancy of an American, which adds up to 27,375 apples over the course of a lifetime. The average person can eat one apple in eight bites. 8 × 27,375 = 219,000. That's a lot of bites.

We get a lot of chances to take a bite of something that's good for us. If you miss a bite of an apple, or bite the wrong way, or refuse to bite because the last one revealed a worm (or worse, half a worm), the next day provides another opportunity to take more bites. The next apple is always right around the corner.

Bruce was a hard-driving founder and CEO with a need to be successful. He'd built a successful business that took up most of his time and attention with a demanding schedule of meetings, travel, and troubleshooting. Bruce was tired of the grind but he struggled with the idea of selling his business. He liked being active and the stimulation of problem-solving, but the constant demands of leadership were driving him crazy and taking up all his waking hours. He didn't know what to do. Without realizing it, his motivation for going to work every day became based on habit instead of desire and served to distract him from other aspects of his life that weren't going so well. His second marriage was failing, and he barely talked to his children.

The business, to him, was his big success, the thing that made him a hero. He was afraid his business wouldn't survive without him, and since it represented the validation he'd chased all his life, giving it up meant, in his mind, the end of his story. He couldn't imagine what could come next. He hadn't given himself any time or desire to think about future roles or projects. He was afraid his future would be nothing but idleness, arguments, and a slow slide toward irrelevance.

To Bruce, his business had become his identity. He was Luke Skywalker saving the galaxy, and his company was his lightsaber. He didn't know who he'd be without it. Without that identity, he thought he'd lose something essential about himself.

Focusing on change's potential losses rather than gains fits nicely with Tony Robbins's discussion of scarcity mindset, or the idea there are only so many chances you're going to get in life, so many decisions you'll be able to make, so many times you can pivot after mistakes before all the chances are spent. Therefore, you, as the hero of this journey, have to be perfect, too. But Luke Skywalker wasn't perfect. He ended up on the wrong side of the Death Star, in a trash compactor. Hell, he didn't even believe in the Force in the beginning.

To some extent, we have to forgive ourselves for our constant scarcity mindsets, too. Prioritizing fear and what we might not have tomorrow has been hardwired into our biology as animals. It's a survival mechanism. Why is it that my dog, Quint, sits at my feet after eating a giant meal and begs? He's about to pop and yet he still wants the chicken I'm making. His brain is wired for scarcity even though he's never in his life skipped a meal. As a dog, he is still controlled by the ancient part of his brain that tells him to get what food he can when he can so his body can survive the next famine.

As humans in an industrialized country, the majority of us rarely have to worry about famine, yet our brains still like to focus on preventing hurts and mistakes that could threaten our survival. It is an act of effort and courage to step away from that and step into a place of abundance and positivity where every iteration of ourselves contributes to our whole story.

Arnold Schwarzenegger looks and acts the part of a real-world hero to his admirers, but his current influence is the result of many iterations of himself, from immigrant, to world class bodybuilder, to A-list actor, to governor of California, to motivational speaker. He's not one to rest on his laurels, and he's not one to get stuck in his old story.

The level of your success in any one realm doesn't matter; what matters is not trapping your life in a binary of "this is the right thing to do" and "this is the wrong thing to do." There are many chances in life to create, revise, and repair yourself. To revisit decisions you've made and choose a different path. To take another bite of the apple.

Life isn't two dimensional, and it doesn't follow a straight line. No one decision proscribes a life. The path taken or not taken doesn't define you. You define the path. And you define the lesson you take from traveling it.

At some point, we have to face the fact we can't do it all. Even

Amazon CEO Jeff Bezos, one of the richest and most successful people in the world, found he only had twenty-four hours in a day and other paths he wanted to follow. Actor Ryan Gosling, at the height of his popularity and demand, decided he wanted to take a step back and focus on his family. Both of these people had to make a shift in how they saw themselves.

Fictional stories only follow a piece of a life, one great adventure. They don't cover what came before that adventure, or what comes afterward, and everything ties up neatly at the end. But in real life, as in real business dealings, there are natural role shifts. We don't go on one adventure, but many. Each chapter is its own story, with its own challenges, lessons, and achievements—and they don't always end so neatly.

Turning the last page of one chapter leads you immediately to the next. Somehow, though, we are scared to death of the pause between ending one story and starting the next. To figure out if you're ready to turn the page, ask yourself this: am I enjoying any of this? Give yourself time to reflect on what you actually like about the situation you're in. Is the weight of the good worth the weight of the bad? Can you get the things you like by doing something else?

We already know that life is iterative. Even if we don't want to iterate with it, it will iterate without us. It plays the game whether we step on the field or not. Evolution of self-concept is also iterative. Realizing the story of your biggest accomplishment may only be the story of *one* big accomplishment frees you to create other stories. All Luke Skywalkers eventually become Yodas. The apprentice becomes the master. Life experience and knowledge build over time, and age makes us want to slow down and let the young and energetic take over. There's nothing wrong with becoming a serial entrepreneur, an angel investor, or the wise industry mentor. Selling a business and handing it off to the next generation doesn't mean you also hand off your values or who you are. All it does is redefine what those values look like in action.

Each stage of a life is a new chapter and opens up different areas of your life to creation, revision, and repair. Maybe you want to improve your physical health. Maybe you want to take up a side business upcycling antiques. Maybe you would just like time to figure out what the hell you like to do because your 120-hour workweeks didn't allow room for that kind of personal growth.

Here's another way of thinking about it. Visualize a long hallway with a lot of doors, like something you'd find in a large hotel. Some are partially open and you can peek through to the other side. Some are closed but open easily when you turn the handle. Some are stuck and you have to put your shoulder into the door to budge it. Some are locked with no key in sight. Once you get beyond a door, you find another hallway with more doors in similar states of openness and you start pressing on those doors.

LIFE ISN'T DO OR DIE WITH ONLY ONE WAY TO THREAD THE NEEDLE.

Life is a series of pressing on doors to figure out which ones will open for you and which ones you actually want to enter. It's an exploration of options that leads to more options. Children have no problem embracing this kind of exploration. Imagine a five-year-old in a hallway full of doors that lead to other doors. Every door that could be opened would be. Every hallway would be run down. If some of the doors opened to elevators, every button would be pressed. And within ten minutes, the five-year-old would be a major influencer on his own YouTube channel. Whereas an adult would spend hours in that initial hallway, trying to decide which door they should open first.

People get stuck on the threshold of making a life shift—

personally, professionally, romantically—because they are afraid to see who they are on the other side of that door. Or, they are afraid it's the wrong door, and crossing over to this new room means they can't go back if they don't like it. They are afraid this door isn't the one they *should* be going through to live up to who they *should* be. So they beat their heads against the door instead, waiting for divine inspiration to tell them where to go, exhausting themselves in the process. Or they retreat from the door entirely because they don't want to take the risk of opening it the wrong way. Running in place or not running at all. Either choice leads to unhappiness.

Staying on a path that makes you unhappy, or not choosing a path at all because it *might* make you unhappy, is no way to live a good, fulfilling life.

Bruce would eventually get so tired of running he was forced to shift his frame of identity. He sold his business, spends more time with his family, and is now experimenting with leadership roles in his community. And he's much, much happier.

You are more than the roles you've chosen. Roles are creations that get revised and repaired over time. A role is just a role, a set of tasks that others can do equally well or better. If the door you chose makes you feel better, keep going through those types of doors. If going through a door makes you feel worse, by all means, choose another one to try.

SUCCESS IS SOMETHING YOU DO, NOT SOMETHING YOU ARE. FAILURE IS THE SAME.

Life is not black and white. There isn't a right and wrong way to be. To do things. To get there. There are 1,001 choices you can make—1,001 bites of the apple. There's no good reason to get stuck on just one choice, one chance, as the event that will make or break you.

Bruce's identity rested on a preconception of who he was supposed to be, the leader of the company he'd created. To free himself to step into his next chapter, he first had to let go of the notion—a notion he'd created—that Bruce the Badass Business Guy was the best version of himself, and without this role he'd be somehow diminished.

There was never supposed to be a perfect version of you. Even if there was, it was never your burden to carry. Decisions aren't final. They are not a zero sum, win/lose game. Decisions don't have to be perfect because you'll get a lot of them in your life. And since you also don't have as much control over the outcome as you think you do, it only helps to let go of that perfection expectation—or what I like to call perfexpectation—sooner rather than later.

If the first step to an unbreakable you is realizing life is iterative, the next step is letting go.

PART 2

LETTING GO

CHAPTER 5

YOU CAN'T SOLVE THE EQUATION WHEN YOU'RE ONE OF THE NUMBERS

I INTRODUCED RON, WHO'D BEEN STRUGGLING BY HIMSELF with his marriage troubles for years, to a couple's counselor. One day, the counselor said, "Ron, you can live life any way you want, you just have to choose what that way is." This shifted his frame.

"My God," he told me later, "if we're going to make this relationship work, there's some shit that has to change. And if we're not going to make it work, that's okay, too." He finally saw he could move in a direction and live life the way he thought it should be lived. Here was a high-powered CEO, confident in his abilities, who had spent years living in his equation, not seeing the numbers. All it took was one conversation with another person to flip his perspective and set him up for a solution.

Many of us carry the idea that we are the only ones who can

get us to the next step in our development. It's all on our shoulders. We have to figure it all out in the dark, alone in a corner, because we feel vulnerable when others see the messiness of our growth, or we feel ashamed to get help. We think we need to pull ourselves up by our bootstraps alone. But you can't solve the equation when you're one of the numbers. To explain what that means, try this.

Remember algebra? Where X plus Y equals Z? As one human in a life equation full of variables, we can only be X. As X, we can't always see what Y is, or how to solve for Z. We can't see the equation we live in. Someone needs to come in from outside, who's not a number in that equation, to explain all the variables and help us solve the problem.

When you are deep inside a problem, you can't see all its moving parts. You can't see what you can't see when you are the one in motion.

At the peak of their performance, athletes know what to do and are extremely good at their chosen sport. They know how to eat and exercise. They know how much time they need to dedicate to practice to win. So why do they keep a more experienced trainer around to coach them?

Professional athletes—the successful ones—know they have blind spots because of their hyperfocus on their training. The athlete knows what to do physically, they feel when they're on or off, but they can't always see exactly how they're getting it right or wrong. They may not know the latest science on diet and exercise for their sport, or the strengths and weaknesses of their latest competition. They may not know how to handle the mental challenges of a bad loss, or how to best recover from certain injuries. They know they need help to see the bigger picture, an outside set of eyes.

We have to shift our frame from being a prodigy to that of a protégé. We have to swallow our pride and let go of a solo journey to solving our problems. We have to let others in, whether that's family, friends, mental health professionals, or an actual personal trainer to help us grow into the next best version of ourselves.

Any kind of change, no matter what, is going to hurt. Growing pains, both literal and figurative, are a fact of life. When a child's body stretches to become an adult, there are all sorts of bone-deep aches as internal structures change at their most basic level. It hurts—but it's a fantastic hurt. Growing pains show things are progressing the way they should.

What sucks about many self-help books is they never include the chapters where it hurts. They gloss over the fact that making big changes to your mind takes as much dedication and pain as making big changes to your body. What's more, you can't easily make mental shifts on your own. Like athletic coaches, life coaches and other professionals give you direction on how to make changes safely. There are too many variables to keep track of without help.

Life is not only an iterative process, it's a collaborative process. Even at the last gasp of life we have pallbearers to carry us to the grave. Why pretend we don't need support during the rest of our lives as well? Why would we expect our lives to be different from our deaths?

One of the last things we need to let go of is that life can be free from pain. That we always have control over how our bodies and minds stretch and grow. That our stories can avoid conflict.

GROWTH AND CHANGE HURTS, BUT WE CAN'T LET THAT HURT SILENCE US.

The story of any Olympic athlete contains pain. That's how they win gold—by overcoming their fear of letting people in so those people can help them find solutions and grow.

We must let go of the expectation that, win or lose, we achieve our outcomes alone. Intuitively. Independently. Isolated. As Brené Brown says in *Rising Strong: The Reckoning. The Rumble. The Revolution.*, "We don't have to do it all alone. We were never meant to." That internal narrative doesn't actually exist in the real world. And it can be damaging to follow.

Letting go means to let go of the old internal narratives, that you always have control over the trajectory of your own story. Part of those old narratives is thinking self-improvement needs to be done on your own. That it hinges on a right and wrong choice. That the choices we make won't cause us some hurt, some discomfort.

Pain we can either face or let scar us.

CHAPTER 6

THE TRUTH CAN HURT BUT NOT FACING IT CAN SCAR

WHEN I WORKED FOR AN INNER-CITY INPATIENT HOSPITAL in Boston, I met Hermione. The police had brought her in involuntarily so she could sober up after yelling at pedestrians and throwing a rock through a store window. Her clothes were torn and dirty. She was in her forties, unemployed, and had been homeless for a number of years. Addicted to methamphetamines, she suffered from paranoid thoughts. Her family was desperate to get her into services so she could face her addiction issues but they were at the point of giving up on her. It didn't take an expert to see she wasn't doing well.

I talked with her, offered her entry into substance-recovery programs, which included reliable healthcare and a stable, safe place to start exiting homelessness. But Hermione refused to take those options. She'd built up a rationale for why she needed the drugs. They were the only thing that helped her chronic sinus problem.

Let me fill in her backstory a little. Hermione was smart. She had a master's degree. She'd worked in the tech industry. Yet she'd created a reason why she needed to keep going on this destructive path, even though it had cost her everything. She was more afraid to recognize she had addiction issues and take steps to change than to stay where she was. Facing the truth—which required admitting who she was and how little control she had over her own life at that point—was too painful.

Whether we realize it or not, at times we all indulge in a fantasy of how things are going to go. It may not feel that way at the moment, but we hold onto the idea that we will perfectly, flawlessly, independently navigate our decisions to arrive at this ideal version of ourselves. The final, best version. But this ideal version is a fantasy. And it hurts to face the fact we are holding our real selves to standards that don't often occur in the gray areas of lived life.

The truth hurts. It is uncomfortable. It's something that you have to go through, like spilling a drink on yourself in front of a date or setting a broken bone. The hurt impacts you and leaves an impression, but hurt doesn't last forever. With time, the evidence of the wound fades completely; sometimes it scars, leaving proof of healing.

Scars are signs of deep damage. You've healed, but incompletely. And the evidence is with you forever, permanent and indelible, sometimes giving you a twinge if you move the wrong way. For Hermione, her scars caused irreparable harm. Homelessness brought on other health issues, other risks to her mental health. Her continued slide downhill was hard to watch.

At some point you *will* have to face the unrealistic expectations you've put on yourself after the damage has been done. Or you will never face it, and life will forever feel like some big mystery you can't figure out.

The first step on any path of recovery is accepting that you have a problem. Rationalizations are only a temporary hiding place; they don't help your situation change. So why do people avoid the truth until they scar themselves with repeated unhealthy behaviors?

We like to repress feelings and thoughts that are uncomfortable and don't fit the ideal version of us. Hermione most likely started her adult life thinking drugs were bad. That people with addictions were bad. When she fell into this problem herself, she couldn't face that drug use was now part of her identity. At that moment, keeping on her current path, even a destructive one, was more comfortable than seeing herself as "bad" and changing direction.

The actual prospect of change is so scary we can't see the other side of it, so we invent reasons to stay exactly where we are. It's the classic "better the devil you know than the one you don't" scenario.

We don't always know where our scars are. Often, we need other people or new circumstances to dig through the narrative and to uncover our pain points and then help us navigate the impulse to avoid facing them.

Luna was in her late twenties and had never had sex, much like Barry mentioned earlier. She told herself romantic relationships weren't important right now. She was too busy with her education and career. She hadn't found the right person. She didn't want to go through the hassle. Only when Luna turned around one day and realized she was twenty-seven and had never been in a relationship—and *wanted* to be in a relationship—did she seek out help. The pain under Luna's narrative was an anxiety built since childhood surrounding romantic unknowns. It's not that she was too busy to date; she was too afraid of exploring her own sexuality. And, unsurprisingly, too afraid of getting that first experience wrong.

We create narratives to avoid facing the pain of a truth, but avoiding the truth doesn't get rid of our reality, a reality that will scar us anyway if left unchanged. It's like covering your eyes to escape an oncoming car.

HIDING FROM HURT ONLY CREATES MORE SCARS.

The truth hurts but not facing it scars. Thinking we aren't supposed to have certain problems because they don't fit the identity we've imagined for ourselves is just another fantasy. A way to escape and hide from reality. Facing it means recognizing our pain and the problems it causes, which allows us to move forward. If we could let go of our fantasies of who we think we are supposed to be, we could start repairing our real lives. To recognize you have a problem you're not supposed to have requires an identity shift, and often we need help to sort out this cognitive dissonance between who we are and who we *think* we are.

Irrational rationalizations keep us in place because, to some extent, we want them to. People love to rationalize to justify their fear. I can't go on this trip because my mom might need me. I can't afford to walk away from this job that's stressing me out. If I go on that date, they might reject me because of my past, so I'm saving myself from more pain. Repressed feelings and thoughts burn in the back of our brains, even as we sabotage what's healthy for us. But we can't sit on our feelings forever. They are connected to the real version of ourselves, the flawed version with all the cracks.

At some point, though, we have to take the risk that we can work with our flaws and carve out something beautiful anyway. From time to time, that means letting go of a path we don't need to be on.

CHAPTER 7

SOMETIMES IT'S NOT GIVING UP, IT'S LETTING GO

I'M LARGELY A COMPLETIST WHEN IT COMES TO BOOKS, though I do allow myself to skim and skip chapters that don't interest me. Sometimes, I'll read a book in spurts, a chapter now and then. I'm more thoughtful and judicious about how I spend my reading energy now, but I wasn't so free with my expectations when I was in my twenties.

I was in medical school when I finally read Ayn Rand's massive pro-capitalist thought experiment *Atlas Shrugged*. I'd tried reading it in high school but couldn't get through it. Then again in college, but just couldn't get into it. The book sat on my shelf for years, mocking me, until the mental pressures of medical school prompted me to pick it up again. The bombardment of dense science and anatomy classes made me want to read anything else, and Ayn Rand was that anything. It took me a year and a half. I'll never forget when I finished it, sitting under a tree by a lake in Tallahassee, Florida. I got to the last sentence, closed the cover, put the book down, and reflected for a moment. Then, out loud, I let out a slow, "What. The. Hell." While the book has been heralded as an American classic, it didn't land with me. I'd never get that time back in my life.

I'd known I didn't like the book before I got to the end, but at some point I was three hundred pages in and felt I was in too deep to quit. I'd tried to read it several times and it felt like failure to give up once more. Eventually, I was a thousand pages in and thought I was now committed to finish, that somehow it would pay off. It didn't.

We don't quit painful paths because we feel like we've committed too much time, too much energy, and far too many resources to them already. The fear of what comes next, the fear of change and uncertainty and getting to know a different path, is too great. The pain point is too buried under the history of that journey, and the expectations of where that journey will end.

To call back to an earlier chapter, you can't solve the equation when one of the numbers is beating your head against the wall. You can't find the solution when you don't have all the numbers, either. If you don't have the resources or abilities to get the healthy outcomes you want, sometimes walking away is the best option.

I see too many people who stay too long in relationships that aren't working. They stay too long in jobs. They stay too long on a path they think will lead them to perfection, or to their ideal life. This is the path they are supposed to be on, they reason. To stop going down this path feels like failure, an end to their story, especially if they've committed a lot of time and energy to it. It's the sunk cost fallacy of business. The idea is that the company's put too much money and too many resources into this initiative to back out now and "lose" that expenditure. Gamblers also experience the impulse to keep going when they're in a hole, thinking the only way they can recoup their losses is to keep betting on a big future payoff. But how much more money and resources are going to be thrown at a problem that doesn't have a visible solution? What if that cost was invested in another direction? Another solution?

When you start to feel like the cost you're paying is hurting you rather than helping you, it may not be giving up, but just time to let go.

I want to reframe the failure narrative here. Knowing when to retreat is not a performance flaw. It's okay to let go of expectations and what you thought your path should be. Life is not predetermined. Fate is a belief, not fact. If you hung your hat on this particular outcome, well, why can't you pick your hat up as you head out the door?

People can't bear the pain of doubt. Doubting whether they're on a good path is the same. They think they shouldn't even have questions or concerns about what they are doing, as if their ideal self would accuse them of thought crimes.

HOLDING TO A PATH THAT ISN'T LEADING YOU ANYWHERE BUT TO A CLIFF HOLDS YOUR RESOURCES HOSTAGE.

Your money, your emotions, your energy, your better tomorrow—everything is chained down by an expectation because it feels icky to let that go.

One of my favorite illustrative stories is the monkey with its hand in a box. To catch a monkey, hunters put a piece of fruit into a box with a small hole cut in the top and anchor the box to the ground. The monkey smells the fruit, puts its hand in the box to grab it, and finds its fist around the fruit is too big to go back through the hole. The monkey is now trapped, not by any physical ropes or chains, but because it doesn't want to open its hand and lose its prize. The monkey hangs onto the fruit even when the hunters arrive, more afraid to let go of food and its perceived gain than the humans coming toward it. The end result, of course, isn't good for the monkey.

I don't know if that story is true or not, but I do know that letting go when something isn't working doesn't always save your life, but it can save your potential happiness. What's the harm in letting go? What could be the potential benefits?

You aren't supposed to have it all figured out. To move forward, you first must let go of the narrative that paths should be painless or see a painful path through out of some vague sense that it will be worth it. Because there's no rule that says there's a reward for pain. Sometimes it's just more pain.

Payoffs do not correlate to the amount of effort you invest. You don't have to stay on paths that lead you to more scars rather than less, or that don't feel like they're leading anywhere. Leaving a path that is too painful or too stagnant does not make you a failure; it makes you a decision-maker. Someone who can jump in the ocean and swim toward something potentially better.

Once we let go of the idea that there's a perfect path, a perfect way to do things, a perfect us, we can start to accept the fact, no matter our path or how we walk it, that we've always been good enough.

PART 3

BEING GOOD ENOUGH

CHAPTER 8

A.I.G.E. SYNDROME

AM I GOOD ENOUGH?

INDIANA WAS AN EXTREME PERFORMER. HE COULD BE 87 percent proficient at something but focus on the 13 percent that needed improvement. He'd actually say that to me: "I'm 87 percent there. I need to work on the other 13 percent to be successful."

An entrepreneur in his early thirties, Indiana was just starting to see the fruits of his early labors pay off. He'd worked his ass off in his twenties doing incredible things, and after only a decade or so he had a comfortable income coming through the door. He'd done an incredible thing but was starting to feel the daily grind of it all as those large numbers, while impressive, didn't match up to the spectacular amounts he thought he should be making at that point.

Since I was a few chapters ahead of Indiana in my life story, I could see how his efforts would springboard him to a stunning future at a relatively young age. But Indiana, himself, had lost perspective of how hard he'd worked and what he'd already accomplished. Every one of his accomplishments didn't measure up to those of others. There was a guy who chartered private jets. There was one who hung out with Swiss models. Here was a guy who owned a mansion in Italy. Here was one who had a yacht. In Indiana's eyes, everyone else was doing better than him. Why wasn't he there yet? Where were his Swiss models? His private jets? His boats? How could he be missing the mark by so much?

Indiana, it seemed, was addicted to moving the goalpost for himself. Since his goalpost was never close enough for him to score, he couldn't win. He was always looking up the ladder at how far he had to go, not down at the rungs he'd already climbed. All he could see were his deficits.

Not achieving 13 percent at a thing means you are still achieving 87 percent of it. The amount you are successful vastly outnumbers where you aren't. Sure, focusing on where we want to improve might goad us to get better, but do we always need to achieve at 100 percent?

Olympic athletes compete without expecting to get perfect tens. They show up, concentrating on what they do best, and try to be the best, if only for a moment. Sometimes they win gold, sometimes bronze; sometimes they don't win anything at all except the glory of getting to the Games. That's how it goes. Athletes compete because they know the reality: a gold medal is never earned through perfect tens.

Getting perfect tens, going at 100 percent—that's not how life works. Constantly focusing on our perceived shortcomings causes us to miss out on the work we've already done. How far we've already made it. And the wins we can get with less-than-perfect numbers.

"Okay," I said, "tell me about the Swiss models, Indiana. What are they doing? Where are you going with them? What's that look like?" I was attempting to dispel the fantasy expectations he'd created—the flashy idea that he'd only be successful when he could afford a private jet with Swiss models drinking champagne and eating caviar. "Who is in your life that you care about sharing those experiences with? Who are you creating these memories for?" Indiana couldn't explain that part.

When Indiana followed his expectations to their logical conclusion, he realized he'd made a hollow vision for himself. Sure, it looked cool. Models and jets would be bragging rights and make a good Instagram photo or two, but would that fulfill him in the long run? Since a meaningful partner was also one of Indiana's goals, his priorities didn't seem to match up. He wasn't imagining any kind of long-term emotional payoff; his self-questioning—am I good enough?—came down to a fear of missing out.

If A.I.G.E. syndrome—constantly questioning, "Am I good enough?"—churns on the fear of missing out, its causes are rooted in doubt. You're supposed to be a doctor or a lawyer or have this level of income and this big a house and this type of car. You're supposed to hang out with models and have a model family. That's what you hold yourself up to. But do you ever stop to ask where these images come from?

We get feedback from our social microcosm. That's our family. That's our schooling. That's carefully curated Instagram photos, TikTok videos, and LinkedIn posts. That's opinion pieces and pundits and podcasts. All those voices combine to create an echo chamber of the society we live in. A narrative that validates and judges our decisions. Something we come to admire, then envy, then are desperate to copy.

Admiration is respecting a quality in another. We may or may not want it for ourselves, but we respect it. Envy is a quality we want because it makes us feel less than to not have it. For example, I admire people who are at ease with networking. I'm not one of them. It would be a nice skill to have, but it's not a comparison. Good networkers are not better people because they display this quality and I don't. If I felt envious, I would think I'm a second-class citizen in my own life, making a value judgment about myself and most likely the networkers, that I was somehow less than because their skill does not come naturally to me. Worse, it would be pulling the networkers down to make myself feel better. I'd tell myself they're brown-nosers, self-absorbed, phony, or any other narrative that helped soothe that self-imposed hurt. But those stories don't make me any better and are certainly not kind to me or to them.

External feedback tells us what we should be doing and what our lives should look like. It provides the model for the fantasy version of ourselves. But how would accomplishing this endless list of things make you happy? You, right now, living your life? What do they get you?

IF GETTING EVERYTHING WE THOUGHT WE WANTED WAS THE KEY TO HAPPINESS, THEN THERE WOULDN'T BE ANY FAMOUS PEOPLE IN REHAB.

Everyone who achieved renown and financial success would be happy. But sometimes they aren't.

Goals for goals' sake, without meaningful relevance to your emotional life, will never fulfill you. Checking off empty boxes does not mean they are any less hollow. You'll find yourself looking for the next empty checkbox, that last 13 percent...5 percent...1 percent...thinking, "If I just check *this* off, then I'm there! I'll feel whole! I'll finally be good enough and my life can finally begin!"

It's worth it to note, when lives end, obituaries list off what people did in life, not what they didn't do.

Here's something I tell all my high performers: if your goal is to run a marathon, run it and be done. You don't have to continue beating yourself up for your time or your pace if the goal was to just complete one marathon. You don't need to languish and wallow in criteria that weren't attached to your original goal, or hold yourself to standards that weren't even on the board when you started.

You don't need to check off goals for the sake of checking off goals without thinking about what those goals are, or how they'll move the needle. You can make yourself a little crazy by creating expectations of what the outcome of your race is supposed to be, especially if you make those expectations after you run it. The goal of the marathon gives way to minutia. It's not enough anymore to just run a marathon. Now you have to run it in a certain time, in a certain way. You move the goalpost on yourself. Completing the marathon is no longer enough. You feel like a failure.

But what if, instead of adding goals to bloat your original one, you took on one goal at a time? One marathon. Then a marathon done in a better time. Then a triathlon. The first marathon is now an entry point to a string of goals that can be reached more realistically. You don't have to be everything, everywhere, all at once to people.

Dr. Jones was a good doctor. He possessed a tremendous amount of education and experience. But even the best of us can have imposter syndrome in any given encounter. Any kind of friction in his practice led him to second-guess his decisions. He became hesitant about calling specialists to consult on his cases. Was this a seizure or heart disease? Should he call the neurologist or the cardiologist? Was this the right time to bring in the cardiologist or did the patient just need to go on blood pressure medication for a while and lose weight? Should he bug his busy colleagues with this? He would feel his A.I.G.E. syndrome whenever he wondered, "Am I a good doctor?"

At some point, Dr. Jones had to realize that his doubt wasn't caused by what was happening in the exam room; it was happening in his head. The unhappy patient wasn't about him. The impatient, overworked colleague wasn't about him, either. He was still a very good doctor. He was still doing what was best for his patients. He should consult with these specialists. He should follow up on all potential causes of disease. His doubt was all related to trying to read the tea leaves, to predict the future, and follow the path of least resistance. To regain his confidence, he had to practice telling himself he was good enough.

So try it. What have you to lose? Stop and tell yourself, "Hey, I'm pretty great. I'm doing just fine"—the actual work of building yourself up and realizing you're good enough, à la *SNL*'s Stuart Smalley telling his mirror image, "I'm good enough, I'm smart enough, and, gosh darn it, people like me!" The daily aphorisms sound ridiculous, but there's a reason the comical character in front of a mirror still captures our attention.

External images get absorbed into your psyche and become your internal identity—your character, behavior, and values. Your inside values start to be measured by outside values that then define you and give you worth. That's what produces feelings of not being good enough. Those outside values, and your inability to meet them through your checklist of accomplishments, now become your mistakes and the reason you are not fulfilled. Focusing on the "missing" 13 percent obscures the real reason you aren't happy: You don't recognize and accept you're pretty great as you are, even with the flaws in your marble.

CHAPTER 9

YOU'RE NOT THE SUM OF YOUR MISTAKES

HENRY WAS AN ATTORNEY AT A LAW FIRM. SOMETHING HAPpened. He made a mistake with the accounting that cost the firm a chunk of money. He was reprimanded and taken off some cases. Was he fired? No. Did he experience any significant legal consequences? No. Did that one error impair his income and progression through the firm? Yes, for a while. Or at least, it would have been a while if Henry hadn't turned that one event into the monster of his whole career.

Henry struggled to recover from his sense of failure. It derailed the next fifteen years of his life. He distanced himself from his partners and his family. He told himself he'd never be able to bounce back from that fall from grace. He felt he'd screwed up his perfect path and he was now tainted. He felt he was the sum of his mistakes, so his mistakes now formed the basis for who he was and what he could do. They had become the sum of *him*.

We do have to account for our mistakes. We may have to apologize, pay reparations, even do some jail time. But our mistakes are the same ones millions of other people make every day, too. For all our efforts, we can't always avoid them.

We only amputate our ability to bounce back if we, ourselves, turn a relatively small mistake in the whole scheme of the universe into something with cosmic impact that we cannot recover from. Do we conceive of this mistake as kicking up some dust, or is it a planet-sized asteroid that destroys the world? Is this mistake human-sized, or larger than life? What's the story we tell about it?

Objectively, there are very few world-destroying decisions a human can make. Our mistakes are mostly contained within our own lives. They don't last forever. What's more, though we might blow a mistake out of proportion because of what others might think, what others really think has nothing to do with our mistakes. In fact, they may not see our mistakes at all.

The *Mona Lisa* is Leonardo da Vinci's defining work. It's considered by some art critics and historians as the greatest work of art ever created. But it may surprise you to know da Vinci never displayed it publicly in his lifetime. It was discovered after his death. He'd worked on this painting for sixteen years and never brought it out of his studio.

Who are you to assume your version of good enough is the right one? If the *Mona Lisa* has any flaws, no one sees them, or if they do, they only add to the mystique of the painting. But I bet if da Vinci were still alive, he'd see many. He'd still be hiding it under his bed, making adjustments every day, trying to get that smile just right. Perhaps, in his mind, the *Mona Lisa* was never good enough. It always had mistakes. And the sum of those mistakes made it unfit to share. The world would have been so much the poorer if da Vinci had had his way and the *Mona Lisa* never saw the light of day.

Sometimes, it isn't our perception that matters. The product of our creativity—a painting, a song, a film, a company—is made for the world. So, it needs to be put into that world so others can interpret and, yes, critique it. The sharing is part of the accomplishment, for what else will inspire and be our legacy? Would da Vinci have felt better about displaying the *Mona Lisa* in his lifetime if he had known how much it would mean to humanity? I'd like to think so.

Accomplishment isn't defined by asking, is this good enough? Or, is this perfect? It is defined by asking, is this inspiring?

We don't need perfection to inspire. But we sometimes get into the rut of thinking we do. Here's a more modern example. A story that may look more familiar to us.

Harrison's mother set high expectations of financial success, constantly beating its importance into him: to be somebody you have to make money. It was paramount to everything else and made her a bit cold and distant to him as a child. The lesson was reinforced by a father who died young and didn't have a lot to his name. Because of this, his father's end of life was a struggle. Not a lot of creature comforts, lacking access to good healthcare or support, just existing until he died.

It was a two-punch lesson for Harrison. Money became his north star, and he threw himself into his business and got that money. But the effort, and the fear of losing what he'd gained, was killing him in terms of the time and energy he put into it. Eventually, he couldn't keep up that level of energy anymore. He stopped caring as much about the day-to-day. He made more mistakes. He yelled at his employees. The other leaders in the company started pulling him aside and asking what was up. He was getting older and was having trouble physically and mentally keeping up. And he didn't really want to. But, he thought he had to keep that mantle of "successful businessman." To Harrison, a successful businessman equaled a successful person. He couldn't or didn't have time to think of an alternative definition of success.

The only path to life he could see was the one his parents had taught him, each in their own way. He had to be successful in business so he could be financially stable. Business was the one place everything made sense. That's where he got his validation that he was doing a good job.

To change, Harrison had to get to a place of, "I'm okay. I'm enough. I don't need my business to tell me I'm a good person." He had to forgive himself for not endlessly living up to his mother's expectations, and accept that his mistakes didn't need to define who he was in the present or who he'd be in the future.

You are not the sum of your mistakes. You don't have to live in a palace of guilt and shame forever. Yes, in the past you were not the best version of yourself. Yes, you caused pain and maybe a few scars. But those things you did? Those were human-sized mistakes. Most of what we do are human-sized mistakes. They are not planet-sized. Getting a divorce or selling a business or yelling at someone when you were drunk does not end the world or shift the dynamic of the universe. They only affect us and a few people around us, and only for a time. In and of themselves, mistakes do not permanently damage us. Or make us undeserving. It is our perception of the mistake, the guilt and shame and regret we assign to it, that holds us back.

To repair his life, Harrison had to let go of the root cause of his own pain. He had to let go of the notion of who he was supposed to be, a savvy and successful businessman with everything figured out. In his early sixties, he didn't have to be the road warrior for his company anymore. He didn't have to be where the buck stopped on all major projects. He didn't have to work insane hours. Ultimately, the best decision was to step down from the business and allow someone younger and more energetic to take over.

Once Harrison got to the place of redefining his story, he

could let go of the past and look to his future. Now it all made sense. Focusing more on his connections, figuring out who he is and what he wants for this next chapter of his life, Harrison realized he wasn't Luke Skywalker anymore. He'd taken his hero's journey. Now he'd come back and wanted to rest a bit and step into the role of Yoda, to mentor up-and-coming leaders. And he got to invent what that role looked like. He realized that his vision of perfection, one reinforced over and over throughout his life, was making him miserable and wasn't inspiring anyone, least of all himself. What he realized was who he had become, and the journey he took to get to that happier person, was what inspired.

MISTAKES ARE ROCKS ALONG THE ROAD. YOU GO OVER OR AROUND THEM, THEN YOU MOVE ON.

If you don't pick them up, they don't go with you. You get to move on and redefine who you are. You get to write an act three. You get to change, do something different, and accept the new place you arrive at.

You are good enough. If you don't feel that way now, you will. And not feeling it right now doesn't mean you are broken.

CHAPTER 10

EVERYONE HURTS; NO ONE IS BROKEN

LIKE SO MANY OTHER PEOPLE, MARION'S STORY WAS COMMON. She resorted to doing the things many people do to recover their ego when her marriage started failing. She used alcohol and drugs. She had affairs. Her reliance on substances to get through the day did not make her a very nice person for a number of years. And of course, when the less savory things came to light, the tension in her marriage escalated.

Marion is much better now, more healthy both in body and the way she handles challenges. But she could never forgive herself for the earlier hurts she'd caused when she wasn't so healthy. She couldn't see the progress she'd made, or that she was a different person. She couldn't set healthy boundaries at work or home, feeling she deserved to pay for her mistakes. Her guilt weighed on her, and penance for this guilt was accepting a chronically rotten relationship dynamic that made no one happy.

Marion got stuck in a perpetual cycle of guilt and conflict. She chose to do unhealthy things because they made her feel better and in control. Then she felt guilty about that behavior. Then her husband confronted her when he found out about that behavior, which made Marion feel more out of control. Rinse and repeat. She didn't stop to consider what was good for her; she thought she deserved this punishment because she'd been a driving force for conflict early in their marriage. She thought she was permanently broken, and this is what a broken woman deserved.

To be broken, we must first have an idea of perfection. Somewhere along the line, we broke the potential of our perfect self and stumbled off the path we were supposed to be on. Mistakes, like stumbles and side quests, are not allowed. They don't fit the ideal of a perfect life. To be perfect, we would have to know who we are before we've lived.

What holds people back from thinking they are good enough? From focusing on their accomplishments rather than on their mistakes? From believing flaws are part of the whole?

It's two sides of the same coin. One is the fantasy version of yourself, who you *think* you're supposed to be. Think of this as the novel or film version of yourself, what I call the novelized version, the person you'd be in your own movie—the one with the happy ending. You've got it all figured out. Life is going great. Everyone loves you. Every decision leads you to the best possible outcome. Effortlessly.

We think one day we'll wake up and be this person. That we'll have arrived. All we have to do is do the right things at the right times and all our waiting will culminate in our metamorphosis into this fantasy superhero version of ourselves. Which is a bit ironic, since even the movie superheroes aren't perfect.

If we flip the coin over, we see our real self, the one that makes mistakes or doesn't accomplish what we think it should. The two sides create an unfair comparison game. Since the first side is perfect, the other side—our real self—must be imperfect. The broken version of who we are supposed to be. The real-but-broken version must constantly live up to the novel-but-perfect version.

The constant comparison of our real selves to our novel selves creates an expectation that can never be achieved. We have to be perfect at work. Perfect at school. Perfect at relationships. Perfect at parenting. We can't win the comparison game but we feel we have to keep playing. And playing a losing game over and over gets us more and more disappointed, anxious, and depressed. We get stuck in a loop of unhealthy behavior that affects all aspects of our lives. Eventually, some people become so afraid they might move forward in the wrong direction that they never move forward at all. It creates analysis paralysis, your mind gaming out all the scenarios, trying to choose the one that leads to that impossible win.

No one life decision defines you as a person. If you overanalyze every action before you take it, you don't give yourself a chance to live a full life. You get stuck at one of life's inflection points, forever thinking of which way to go—which way will bring you to a perfect outcome—instead of going.

The reality is, everyone is going to have challenges in their lives. Everyone will make mistakes. Everyone is going to be wounded and hurt by someone, or is going to hurt someone else. So how can you expect yourself to be perfect in an imperfect world?

THINGS WILL BE MESSY BECAUSE LIFE IS MESSY.

I don't care how perfect someone's life looks, no one has it all figured out all the time, or is free from doubt, indecision or pain. The periodic tragedies surrounding public and powerful figures shows us that. Life is a carousel, and no matter which horse you choose you're going to rise and fall.

Everyone hurts; no one is broken. Broken means to stop functioning and have nothing left to contribute or grow from. That's not true for anyone except the dead.

That doesn't mean we are all playing with the same deck of cards when it comes to being hurt and dealing with that hurt. I acknowledge that some seem to have more pain dealt to them than others. But you are not broken because life handed you something that is hard. Nor are you whole because life gave you something easy.

Elsa had everything. Her family had sold their business for over a billion dollars when she was thirty. At sixty, when I met her, all her wants and needs were satisfied. She didn't need to work and hired people to take care of her daily tasks and errands. But she was bored. She didn't have a purpose. "There's nothing for me to do," she lamented, "nothing that challenges me." She was in the evening of her life and didn't know what to do with herself. She had no hurt to challenge her, to give her something to strive against. In a way, Elsa's *lack* of pain became her pain.

Pain and hurt exist for a reason. They are part of the journey. If it doesn't overwhelm us, hurt can make us stronger. It teaches us. Changes us for the better. How do we get stronger with exercise? We're causing repeated damage to the muscle, forcing it to adapt, get stronger, and be more proficient. Athletes know they need to challenge their bodies with weights and stretches and exercise to toughen and strengthen muscles and ligaments and bone. The stronger muscles force the bones to grow at attachment points. This is a big part of why resistance-based exercise is recommended to prevent osteoporosis and bone degeneration as we age.

There's a rare medical condition where people are born without working pain receptors. The people who have this condition don't feel physical pain. They can see their hand on the stovetop but don't feel the heat. They can see a knife slicing into a finger but don't stop the cut before they need stitches. They end up with more severe injuries from everyday nuisances because they don't have the protective mechanism of pain. A lack of pain produces more pain, in this case both physical and emotional.

When I was ten, I had a *Home Alone* moment. Not the one defeating petty criminals with household booby traps, the one toward the middle of the movie, when Kevin sleds down his stairs with a toboggan, sails out the front door, and crashes into a tree. I did that as a kid, too. The thing is, we lived in Florida. No snow. And my toboggan wasn't a solid structure of wood, it was a neon green plastic thing we had gotten during a Christmas trip to Vermont years before. I rode it down the stairs from a second-floor deck, the kind that has a small landing halfway down. And the landing spot? A rocked area underneath the house. I made two successful trips and thought, "This is fantastic! I have to show my dad!"

The third time in front of my father wasn't the charm. I landed hard on my tailbone, and my entire back spasmed so hard I couldn't get up. My dad, a neurosurgeon, asked if I could wiggle my toes. I could, so we didn't think much of it. I couldn't walk for a couple days, but I slowly got better and no problems followed.

I never really thought about the sledding incident again until my twenties when I would occasionally get bad back spasms when I worked out. Then at thirty-six, I woke up one night with horrible spasms. I wanted to take myself to the emergency room, but I couldn't walk. Couldn't breathe, it hurt so bad. Ultimately, my doctors found I had an old compression fracture in one of my vertebrae. "How the hell did you do that at thirty-six?" they asked. But I hadn't done it at thirty-six. It was a mistake I didn't realize was a mistake at ten. An accident that happened when I was experimenting and having fun. I didn't realize that the muscles had inflamed around my spine, tightened up in what doctors call "chronic guarding" to protect the old injury. The constant tension had thrown off my body mechanics for twenty-five years, and at thirty-six the soft tissues couldn't hide it anymore.

I still have some chronic back pain that I manage. That's one of my journeys with hurt. At first, I was angry. The whole thing sucked. Why did I have to live with a chronic pain condition? It wasn't how I thought my life was going to go. I wasn't immune to those feelings of perfection and rightness. But over time, I learned what kinds of exercise I could do and what kinds of maintenance I had to do, like stretching and massage, to keep things working.

We think beating ourselves up for our brokenness will somehow make us better. It doesn't. It prevents us from seeing how we can create, revise, and repair. To step up we have to step away from those old stories and realize there are better, more effective ways to do things that allow us to get on with our lives.

My accident hurt me; it didn't break me. Doubt, mental illness, anxiety, trauma, things you've done to hurt others and what others have done to hurt you—none of it means you are broken. It means you were hurt. It means you experienced another of Life's imperfections. Hurt, even a big hurt, does not mean you can't write your next chapter.

As a doctor, I've seen a lot. We don't have as much control over our destinies as we think we do. Life can be sad. It can kill. It can also be glorious.

Embracing Life's uncertainty is the best way to navigate it. We have to let go of the idea that Life should or will go a certain way and that we do or do not deserve what we're dealt. Life isn't keeping score. If you win, Life doesn't care. If you lose…it also doesn't care. If you hurt less, if you hurt more, it's all the same to Life because Life isn't an entity capable of caring or keeping score. There is no objective end-of-time scoreboard that puts you on a naughty or nice list. We are the ones who make lists, not Life.

Life is also not a director. It doesn't tell us to go stage left or right, or smile more or less. Life doesn't work in wins or losses, rights or wrongs, painful or painless. One good decision doesn't lead to other good decisions. There is no right or wrong path. A thousand little things lead us to disbelief in our own self-worth and capabilities. All the hurts, all the mistakes, all the ways we measure ourselves against others and hold ourselves to a narrative of what we should be—all of it keeps us from recognizing how far we've come and the values that define us as individuals. Instead, we only see the ways we don't measure up, the ways we aren't living our best, the ways we are broken.

The Japanese have several art forms that focus on fracture points and imperfections. One of the most famous is kintsugi, where a mortar made with gold is used to glue a shattered porcelain vase back together. The vase is now considered more beautiful and valuable because of the shimmering fracture lines that speak to the vase's history with hurt.

YOU'RE NOT BROKEN BECAUSE LIFE ISN'T BROKEN.

You're not perfect because Life isn't perfect. The vase was already shattered. The sled already crashed. All we can do is accept that we are going to hurt sometimes. To recover from hurt, to become unbreakable, we have to accept that the sun will rise, the planet will turn, and a new day will arrive. We can have the hope that it will be better tomorrow than it is today, and today is better than yesterday. Our pain may be a part of us, but it doesn't have to define us or dictate what we do next and who we can love.

If you believe you're not good enough, that you are broken, how will you ever form genuine connections with others? How can you show up as an open-hearted, vulnerable version of yourself? Who's open to the complexity and, yes, hurt and mistakes that always happen in a relationship?

While having brunch one morning, an old friend announced she wanted to get a tattoo that said, "Everything you need is inside you." As a doctor, I irreverently thought the phrase sounded like instructions for a surgeon. But the line, popularized by the artist Olivia Steele, has a point. Everything you need is with you. Once you realize you aren't the sum of your mistakes, that you aren't broken, that you're good enough, then you can start to form the genuine healthy connections that most of us want.

PART 4

MAKING CONNECTION

CHAPTER 11

THE HARDEST ROAD IS THE ONE YOU TRAVEL ALONE

STEVE ROGERS WAS IN MY OFFICE LOOKING FOR A NEW PSYchiatrist to check his current bipolar medications. He wanted to know what, exactly, he needed to manage his mental health. But I could smell the marital dysfunction the moment he walked into the room. There was more to this story than adjusting medication.

The more I talked to Steve and got to know him, the more bipolar disorder didn't make a ton of sense. The conflicts with his wife, the previous drug use, the infidelity—it looked like Steve's behavior and relationship issues were more rooted in old traumas than actual disease.

We weaned him off the drugs and did testing to see if he really had bipolar disorder. Negative. So then we could concentrate on the personal conflicts that were bleeding into every aspect of his life. He seemed to be fighting with everyone: his wife, his adult children, his business partners. The medicine Steve needed was to take a step back and focus on why his relationships were falling apart.

Even with help, it took a while for Steve to revise and repair the intimacy he'd lost. There were many backslides and blowups. The fear of not being good enough kept Steve trapped in a bad relationship loop. Physically, he wasn't living alone. Emotionally was another story.

The hardest road is the one you travel alone. And Steve was traveling a hard road. He accepted the idea he'd die alone in a ditch somewhere because no one would be talking to him when he was old. He'd pessimistically accepted that severed connections were his punishment and his forever fate.

We are built for intimate connections, and by this I don't mean intimacy as in sex, but intimacy as in sharing our innermost selves. Healthy relationships can be with anyone and take any form, as long as they are made with an intimate connection that involves mutual sharing. This can be a friendship. A romantic partnership. A familial bond. Anyone whom you feel knows your darkest secrets and is still willing to have you over for Thanksgiving.

We're not built to be alone. It's a clinical disorder when someone doesn't want human beings around for companionship. When we don't make connections, it weighs on us, becoming pathological. We lose the ability to function in our daily lives and each of our relationships by turn.

For the elderly, the twilight of life can be a struggle with a shrinking world, especially if they have a hard time maintaining old connections or forming new ones. If this world shrinks too much, the last phase of life can be one of despair. They end up in hospitals or homeless shelters, going through various government programs. Decades of not making connections has left them alone. I've seen it firsthand, many tragic times.

Even people who go into their later years financially secure, with retirement plans and Social Security, can end on a dark note without connections. There is always loss as we age, not just a loss of loved ones, but also loss of ourselves. Various medical conditions take their toll on our health. Work becomes unmanageable and we are forced to quit. We mourn for the pieces of our identity we have to let go.

If no one is there to help us get past those losses and the grief that comes with them, what then? I see a lot of people depressed because they didn't have anyone to help shoulder the burden of loss and the processing that comes with it. Professional help can mitigate this loss and provide strategies to get through it, but a therapist is not a friend. Not a family. We're not a replacement for someone you can call anytime you've had a bad day.

If you want to repair a relationship, there's just one question to start with: How do we get to a better place?

Relationships are forever a work in progress. Forever changing. We change and grow as people, so of course our relationships change and grow. What connected someone twenty years ago may not be what connects them now.

Periodically, you have to check in with yourself. Does this person still make you feel safe and secure? How do you show up for them? How do they show up for you?

The fear of losing an established but bad relationship is more primordial than feeling like a bad relationship is all we deserve. It's the fear of abandonment and rejection. It's that if I move away from this relationship, move away from this dysfunction, I will be all alone. And the short answer is yes, you will be alone—but only for a time.

People often hold back from new connections because they don't think they're good enough. By holding back, they miss out on the people who are actually showing up in their lives that are good and healthy for them.

We get caught in the trap of expectations. On the journey to revising and repairing our connections, we must learn to let go of the outcome. Things might work out. They might not. They might work out, but not in the way we first thought they should.

Keeping a relationship going at all costs is not the goal. The goal is to be happy, and have a healthy connection, whatever that might look like. Maybe, like Steve, it's just getting to a place where you can be friends with your spouse and everything is financially secure.

Perfect relationships don't work because we never have them. They don't exist, at least not like the fantasies we imagine in our heads. Real relationships are not always 100 percent satisfying—but they allow us to grow.

You can't have everything you want in a relationship. Your partner is another human being who will want to be met in the middle on a lot of things. That's where the strength of connection comes in—you need connection to make compromises. You feel good about being you enough that you can give up or alter a few of your dreams or expectations so the other person can also follow their dreams.

You don't have to never have it, you just can't have it exactly the way you thought you would. You have it to a lesser degree, or at a different time. Compromise is that my partner wants to be healthier so we're not going to buy ice cream every week. Sacrifice, on the other hand, is never eating peanut butter again because your partner is allergic.

IF COMPROMISE IS GIVING SOMETHING UP, SACRIFICE IS NEVER HAVING IT.

Sacrifice, too, comes into relationships, but it should never be something coerced, or something that causes trauma. That's not sacrifice, that's exploitation.

Parents are a good example of healthy sacrifice. Most parents do not jet off all the time to adults-only playgrounds decorated with attractive supermodels. Not if they want to maintain connection with their children. The parents willingly give something up because something else is more important. They sacrifice to get something else they want: true connection with their children. And let's face it, when we get old, unless we're super rich, it isn't supermodels taking care of us, it's our kids. So is giving up the supermodels really a sacrifice after all?

People are fond of saying, "Give the relationship whatever it takes." Connections take compromise. Compromise means change. Don't give up your ability to weigh in on the relationship changes that inevitably come in life.

Steve had a big fight with his wife. After two decades and escalating conflict, he finally had to acknowledge that his marriage was falling apart. He took a big step back and decided to spend some time in another state where the family had property. It was also where his estranged son and grandson lived. He started revising and repairing those connections. He couldn't do anything to fix his marriage at this point, but he could fix this.

He got them into fishing and golf. He helped figure out a family ancestry mystery. He helped his son fix up the property. That little corner of his family is now the happiest and most productive it's ever been. In the end, Steve became the beloved captain of his family's ship (not just America, if you catch the reference), a real force of nature.

THE LESSON HERE IS THAT WHEN WE DO WELL, THOSE AROUND US DO WELL.

Through repairing one relationship, Steve was then able to work on more difficult ones. He could now build on this healthy foundation and apply the skills he'd learned to his marriage. He saw marriage counselors that helped him see what was working with his wife and what wasn't. At the time of writing this book, they are still together.

When you are doing well, you can see your influence. You can take all the energy that's made you successful in other spheres, like business or nonprofit work, and put it into your relationships so they thrive. A Midas touch can be applied anywhere, you just have to reach out your hand.

CHAPTER 12

INTIMACY ISN'T BUILDING YOUR CASTLE WALLS NEXT TO EACH OTHER; IT'S OPENING THE GATES

NATASHA WAS A BADASS BUSINESSWOMAN; SHE ABSOLUTELY crushed it at work. She devoted herself to her job because it was where she could get validation and continue to feel powerful. She wanted to exit her high-powered work but wasn't ready to move on, a little afraid of what came next.

That fear might have been partially due to her marriage. She'd been married for a long time, a few decades, and hung onto the relationship because of her kids, who were young teenagers, and a sense of duty. Distance had grown between her and her husband. They hadn't found a way to communicate with each other, mainly because they couldn't be vulnerable with each other. They both wanted—needed—things so badly but were stuck in an endless round of scorekeeping. She said this; he said that. He did this; she did that. What have you done for me lately? The resentment made them retreat to separate corners of their realm where they set up their own little fiefdoms, living inside individualized castle walls where they felt safe.

For Natasha, the only real security left to her was the abstract connection of marriage. Her identity as a wife provided nothing else in her life that she was happy with. It didn't give her emotional connection or satisfaction. It was only the security of the day-to-day. But that's a house of cards built with only one little flimsy card on the bottom, shaking mightily while it keeps everything else up. Eventually, a breeze blows through and the card tower falls. Then what do you do?

We live behind our castle walls because, if we open up, we think raiders, known and unknown, are going to come in. And if they come in, they are going to take what they want or trash what they don't. Or, they will take over our castle and never leave. Either way, we'll have to face the fact we're not as strong or powerful or capable as we thought we were.

Or, maybe the biggest fear, if we let someone in, past the nice facade that shows outwardly to the world, our visitor will see what's actually going on inside our castle and they won't like the look of it. They'll think less of us. Reject us. Abandon us. Instead of never leaving, they'll never want to stay.

Just because your relationship is long doesn't mean that you can't feel vulnerable and defensive. Natasha and her husband lived together for decades but didn't trust each other. They were no longer working toward common goals. No longer growing. So they stagnated behind their castle walls, unable to grow beyond them. They looked at each other's castle in the distance, thinking, "I'd love to connect with that person," but neither was willing to go outside their own walls to do something about it. That would be too risky.

IT'S HARD TO GIVE PEOPLE THE KEYS TO OUR CASTLES.

It's hard to be vulnerable. It's hard to give people something that shows genuine moments of who we are because we're afraid the other person will judge us for those moments. And we're not free from that fear of rejection and abandonment even with a long-time spouse or our own family members. In fact, the fear can be especially sharp with those we love the most and we want to love us in turn. There are countless adults who say, "I wish I had a better relationship with my parents. I wish my mom and dad had opened up to me. I don't know them as people. I know their collections of eccentricities. I know how they behaved. But I don't know their actual hopes and dreams. They never shared that part of themselves with me."

Castle walls go up because of a thousand small unmet needs. A thousand small situations that get reinterpreted in a way that makes us defensive and puts us behind our walls. They go up, and we can have a difficult time letting people inside of those walls, including the people closest to us.

But intimacy isn't putting your castle walls next to each other; it's opening up the gates. You have to let the other person into your castle and walk around in it for a bit. Let them see all the cobwebs in your corners and dirty socks on the floor. Real intimacy is being able to share not only the good parts of yourself but the messy parts too. The parts you dislike or fear. It goes deep. We all live with doubts and insecurities. Intimacy means you are in a place of comfort, trust, and security, where you can show vulnerabilities without fearing the other person would use them against you.

VULNERABILITY CREATES INTIMACY.

When we invite someone inside our castles, we are being human. Humans aren't just meant to be there for the good times, sharing our successes, accomplishments, and joys. We feel connected when we band together in tough times. Others may have a way of tending to your garden or mending your leaky sink that maybe you don't. Being able to be there for someone and help them through problems creates connections through those shared trials. When people become vulnerable and allow others to see and help, both castles flourish.

In a relationship between two people, both castles have to be open. Sharing vulnerabilities is a two-way street. One-way connections take all you have to give and give nothing back. If the other person only seems to want you to listen to them, but they don't want to listen to you, that's a sign of an unbalanced relationship. Or, if you're the only one who wants to talk but you really don't care what the other person's life is like, that's also a sign.

One-way connections don't make you feel good about being you and what you want. If you take a step back and ask, "How is this relationship benefitting me? How is this relationship making me feel good about life? Do I like talking to this person?" and you have a hard time coming up with positive things to say, then you may be in a relationship that lacks intimacy, where one castle is open and the other closed.

To discover if a relationship is healthy or unhealthy, look to the nature of the connection point. You don't have to be good or perfect, and neither does the other person. But you have to have a good connection point, one made from sharing your inner thoughts and feelings. If you never open up to who you are—your hopes and dreams and fears—if you don't let someone else participate in reaching those dreams and managing those fears, you're an island of one.

After I finished my medical education, I bounced around the country for a while. I've always had a sense of adventure and loved the opportunity to live in all four corners of the country. I traveled to Ireland and New Zealand. I even lived in Scotland. I rode motorcycles. I went skydiving. Career-wise, things were going pretty well. I worked my way up to a head doctor position at a hospital. I looked like I had life by the tail.

But there was a layer of insecurity underneath it all. I was feeling disconnected from people and I struggled to embrace intimacy in my relationships. For all my training and confidence, I couldn't wrap my head around what real intimacy looked like or how to get there. I felt a certain amount of distance and superficiality, even with my brother. We'd always been close but as the years went by and my twenties became my thirties, we couldn't relate to each other on family matters. News, sports, and the weather became topics of conversation. I'd built up castle walls without even realizing it.

One of the first ways I started to let down my walls was with my brother. He was a few years older than me and had kids and got married when he was twenty-three while I went to medical school. He also moved around the country to support his wife's career as a traveling nurse. Finally, they landed back in our hometown in Florida and set down roots. He started his own company and grew it to something sustainable. Meanwhile, the emotional distance, alongside the physical distance, had been growing between us.

One evening, I was sitting by the rooftop pool of my old building, talking on the phone with him on one of our bimonthly calls. I don't remember if this was the first of our regular calls, but it was certainly the most poignant.

"I feel there are times when I've got it and I'm doing good. I have a sense of where I'm going in life. I'm confident and have faith in myself." I paused, looking at the lights shimmer in the pool with the movement of the jets. "But then there are weeks where I feel like I don't have it. I wonder what the hell I'm doing. Am I doing right in my personal life? Am I doing right in my career? Why are things not progressing the way I think they should? I feel like an imposter. Those weeks feel like everything is on a knife's edge and it could all go away." I waited, wondering what my brother would say. I was afraid that if I shared the dark things about myself, the person I shared those things with would either walk away or use those things against me. Such a common fear. So human.

The silence stretched on the other end of the line. "I've had many of those weeks," he finally responded. "There are times you feel like you don't have it. But you surf on those feelings. Those are some of the waves that come with this. You're smart. If you keep your feet on the surfboard, good things will come your way. And you haven't fucked it up yet. Why do you think you will now?"

On the heels of this conversation, I'd go into therapy myself. With a lot of deep work, I moved past my budding pessimism and embraced a place of abundance and positivity. That opened the gates wider and allowed me to let go of my notions of who I was supposed to form relationships with, and made way for some wonderful and surprising connections.

To say "life isn't always good" is to open the gate and let someone in. No one can have any kind of connection—family, friend, or romantic partner—until the flashy exterior of business, travel, and motorcycles is pushed aside to reveal the imperfect human being underneath. My brother isn't a super emotional guy, but I didn't need him to be. I needed him to be able to walk through my walls and listen to my hopes and doubts. And he did the same with me. He opened up about his concerns as a parent, even though I wasn't a parent myself. It made us closer than ever.

You can be on different journeys and still make a connection. You can have different perceived imperfections and still find common solutions. Seeing the others' imperfections can make our own seem less monstrous. You can feel good about being you.

CHAPTER 13

YOU CAN'T EXPECT OTHERS TO FEEL BETTER ABOUT YOU THAN YOU FEEL ABOUT YOU

STEPHEN COLBERT, THE BELOVED LATE-NIGHT HOST, HAS mismatched ears. Sometimes, he points out the atypical one on his show, letting the audience into his castle just a little. Otherwise, you don't even notice his ears because the rest of his face and act are so dynamic. Even if you did notice the discrepancy, you'd probably not care. It wouldn't make you like Colbert less or turn off his show; you'd dismiss that quirk of his appearance and keep being entertained because he'd already built a connection with you as a host as he shared his thoughts and feelings over the years and made you laugh. His wife and family certainly don't seem to care about his ears, either.

You can't expect others to feel better about you than you feel about you. There are going to be people who love or care about you and accept you exactly as you are regardless of your quirks and insecurities. Hell, they probably won't agree on what those are anyway!

How other people feel about us is often a mystery. The things that we want others to love and acknowledge aren't always the things people respond to. We don't get to control how others show up and what they feel or like about us.

Thor was newly sober and hated—*hated*—when others would refuse to drink near him. It took a lot of reflection before he realized he didn't own their reactions. His friends and family wanted to protect him and, while that intent made him uncomfortable, their feelings weren't his to control. His accomplishment, sobriety—what he was proud of and wanted them to respect—was not what they connected with. Instead, his companions connected with his struggle to manage something he could no longer hide.

Healthy relationships can't be based on appearances, either ours or theirs. If someone is occupying an intimate position in your life, mostly because you are afraid of not having someone in that position, that's not a secure relationship. The connection point isn't intimacy, it's fear—the internal fear of being alone, or the external fear of losing what that person means to you. To illustrate this second point, imagine dating a famous actor. Are you in that relationship because of the person, or because of what their status means to you and the people who might see you together?

Intimacy embraces the imperfections of yourself and others. It is not feeling like your worth in a relationship is based on how perfect you are, or how perfect your partner is, or how much you get right. It doesn't care about the fantasy ideal of a "good relationship." Being in a place of "What does this relationship say about me?" is unhealthy. That's not where intimacy lives. You don't want to attach yourself to a person because of a box they check on social media; you want a full person you can open your castle gates to.

FEEL GOOD ABOUT BEING YOU.

What's the stuff you like about you? What are the things that you feel good about? A healthy relationship is built on vulnerability, but it's also built on a sense of self-worth that allows you to trust and feel safe that this other person won't do you irreparable damage because you are strong enough to take it and have the foundation on which to rebuild.

If you go down the road of vulnerability and intimacy, inevitably you'll invite the wrong person into your castle. There's no way to avoid that 100 percent of the time. Having a sense of feeling good about yourself on some core level without expecting the other person to pull your self-esteem up means that when they come in and start mucking about, you know you'll be okay and have the strength to rebuild after you kick them out.

If we expect someone else to make us feel better about ourselves, that person will fail us every time. We set them up for failure. We're setting ourselves up for failure, too. That doesn't mean we have to have all the messy bits figured out, but we do have to have some sense of what we like about ourselves. We have to be intimate with ourselves just as much as with others. All the skeletons in our closets must be acknowledged, and we may need to clean them up a little, but we mustn't think our castle is unlivable or unlovable because they exist. Imagine if Stephen Colbert had let his ears hold him back.

WE HAVE TO BE FRIENDS WITH OURSELVES FIRST BEFORE WE CAN BE FRIENDS WITH OTHERS.

A good intimate connection is one that makes you feel good about being you. Yes, a relationship should also make us want to be better people, but first that family member or lover or friend has to accept you for you, flaws and all. "Every block of stone has a statue inside it and it is the task of the sculptor to discover it," said Michelangelo. Relationships form while you are still an unfinished chunk of marble. Connection starts with showing people what you're working on, not the finished product.

We can't always wait for someone to scale the tower and kiss us awake. Sometimes we have to leave the door open for the serendipitous. If you don't feel good about being you, on some level you run the risk of either, one, never connecting because you're too afraid to open the gates or, two, getting stuck in codependency as you orbit someone else expecting that person to give you self-worth. A relationship can't be built on some future version of you that will hopefully arrive or that the other person will craft. That's a different and often unhealthy dynamic.

Self-worth is a process that has to start from within as we face our flaws and mistakes and accept they are part of our story but not the whole book. We can't let the people we let into our castle be the mortar that holds it together. We still have to have some core concept of who we are—and that who we are doesn't have to be perfect. In fact, people will love you for your perceived imperfections.

Connections are built on our vulnerabilities—our human-sized mistakes. Who wants to be friends with Superman when he's just going to rescue you? You can't have a genuine connection with Superman because Superman will never have a problem he needs your help with. That's why his creators invented kryptonite. So he wouldn't be invulnerable anymore and could have a convincing connection with Lois Lane.

A healthy, successful relationship is built on the security, trust, and comfort that comes from openly being yourself in all of the great and not-so-great ways you go about living your life. There's a mutual agreement that these good and bad behaviors and personality quirks are within each others' acceptable limits of tolerance. Sure, you can improve the bad stuff, but do it because you want to do these improvements to make your life even better, not because these changes will make someone happy or want to stay with you.

Intimate connections are vital. They're part of being human and threaded through our DNA. You will feel deeply alone and isolated without them, and that is a very hard road to walk when you start to open up.

Relationships are built on trust, security, and vulnerability, which together allows us to feel good about opening the gates and letting people in. They will keep us grounded and centered, and help us be better versions of ourselves.

Feeling good about being you is a necessary part of getting to a place of comfort and security. It helps create our intimate connection with ourselves. It allows us to take risks with our castles, because we know we can survive guests that cause us pain.

A castle that never opens its gates may survive but never thrive. If we never open the gates, we may keep out the bad people, but we keep out the good ones too. The ones we may not even expect will look at all we have in our castle, nod, and say, "I like it here. Great castle!"

Figure out what works. Figure out what makes you happy, healthy and whole. No, of course it won't all be perfect. As human beings, we always have bad days. But on the whole, figuring out what you need and want out of a relationship is a start. Then you can reaffirm an old relationship or move into new territory.

Don't delay, because if you wait too long for the perfect time to open your gates, you may miss your chance.

PART 5

DON'T WAIT FOR TOMORROW

CHAPTER 14

CHANGE IS UNDEFEATED

IF YOU EVER WATCHED THE IRREVERENT ADULT CARTOON series *South Park*, or patrolled for memes on the internet too long, you may have encountered the Underpants Gnomes. In the episode, a band of gnomes plots to steal the underwear of the town of South Park. The leader of the band uses a pointer to refer to the different steps of the plan for his diminutive minions to follow:

- Phase 1: Steal Underpants
- Phase 2: ?
- Phase 3: Profit

Obviously, the joke is the gnomes haven't worked out the important Phase 2. But they don't let that stop them in their quest for success.

This may be a funny example, but it does get to the point of not waiting until tomorrow to act. Many of us try to figure out what Phase 2 is before we feel like we're ready to do something.

We think that if we just stand still, we can prevent change, or that change will wait for us, or that we can somehow see it coming and so better prepare for it. But the truth is that change will arrive regardless of whether we see it or whether we want it to.

There is no stopping change. Change is undefeated. And it often arrives sooner than we'd like.

Leia was in her late sixties. She had medical problems, was on various medications, and struggled with a handful of mental health issues, which is why she ended up seeing me. I saw her over the course of a year. She'd worked at the public health office for all her life. Her husband, Han, was in the military, and then also worked for public health, so they had triple pensions. They'd always been savers, squirreling away any extra funds, not spending a lot of money on things that didn't fulfill basic needs. They didn't go anywhere. They never had kids, either by choice or happenstance. Their lives were all work work work.

But Leia had had dreams. At our first meeting, she told me she always wanted to travel. She and her husband put off those adventures until their golden years, after they retired and had the time to see the world at their leisure. But immediately after they signed out of the public health office for the last time at sixty-five, Leia developed health problems. So did her husband. The dream of travel withered along with their bodies. Those broken dreams made Leia vastly unhappy.

I saw Leia twice more before she disappeared for a while, as happens sometimes in the mental health space. Fast-forward a year, and Leia reemerged. I'd almost given up on her ever coming back.

"How's it going?" I asked at our first session after our break.

"Han's dead," she said stoically. I couldn't read her face at first. Leia was good at hiding her emotions. But saying the words released something for her and she started crying. "It wasn't supposed to be this way!" she wailed. "We had so many hopes for the future."

In life, Leia waited for the "opportune moment," as Jack Sparrow would say, but that moment never came. And then it was too late for it to ever come at all. Her story is not uncommon.

To call in Teddy Roosevelt again, nothing starts happening until you get in that arena. You can't wait for the ideal circumstances that will get you a win. You get to be the author of your own change, but only to an extent. You can either execute a course of action and respond to the results, or wait and be reactive and try to play catch-up.

No part of your life is going to be perfectly static. All parts of the universe will change over a long enough period of time. Every moment, the earth moves a little more on its journey. It's not only rotating but also orbiting around the sun, which is orbiting around the Milky Way galaxy. So if you stay in the same place for the next handful of minutes, are you really in the same place? Cosmically speaking, no, you're always moving. As humans on a planet, we are never in the same place twice.

Biologically speaking, we also always move forward. There are billions upon trillions of chemical reactions happening inside your body at all times. Nausea is a common occurrence when people are undergoing chemotherapy. Want to know why? Cancer cells lose their regulatory mechanism and multiply out of control. Chemotherapy targets rapidly dividing cells for this very reason. But the lining of the stomach is also frequently turning over because it is exposed to a very acidic environment all of the time, the one that helps us digest food. In fact, stomach cells regenerate so frequently, it's estimated to only take three to six days to have a whole new lining. So, chemotherapy impairs them just as much as cancer cells and the lining grows "old" and beat up, leading to nausea. Almost every cell of your body has a finite lifespan and is replaced multiple times within the course of one lifetime. You are literally not the person you were a year ago. Even brain cells, which do last a lifetime, change slowly. They are plastic, adapting to stimuli from the environment, both the stimuli we can't control and the ones we can.

Time is a one-way flow, despite what the Marvel Cinematic Universe wants us to believe. Every second is different from the second that happened before it. We are born. We move through life stages. We die.

> **LIFE'S BEGINNING AND THE END ARE ALWAYS THE SAME; IT'S HOW WE CHOOSE TO MOVE THROUGH THE MIDDLE THAT COUNTS.**

The truth is, sometimes you're not going to know exactly what Phase 2 looks like, but you have to dive in anyway if you have any hope of profiting. The secret of the old Ben Franklin adage "Don't put off until tomorrow what you can do today" is this: tomorrow will arrive, whether you want it to or not, but that doesn't mean you have to wait for tomorrow to act. If change is coming anyway, why not make that change something you choose to do now?

You can either accept that change is part of life and engage it or it will change you all the same.

CHAPTER 15

CHANGE NOW OR NOW WILL CHANGE YOU

I WAS HEAVY ALL OF MY CHILDHOOD. WHEN PUBERTY KICKED in, I got a brief reprieve when a lot of the calories I took in went to getting taller, but by the time I was seventeen I was overweight again. I stayed heavy all through college and medical school. When I graduated as a doctor, I was at my heaviest, a whopping two hundred and forty pounds. I was five feet, eight inches tall and totally sedentary.

I moved to Boston and established a primary care doctor who told me point-blank, "Jon, you're the perfect weight—you're just a foot and a half too short." It was a hard thing to hear, and I thought he was an asshole, but he had a good point. I wasn't in control of what was happening to my body anymore. I wasn't putting any effort into keeping it healthy. It took me another year before I did anything, and that's because I got some labs back that showed my liver enzymes weren't happy with my weight. In consultation with my doctor, I knew I was heading toward metabolic syndrome, which is a precursor to diabetes and hypertension and all the things that come with being too heavy for too long. I was only twenty-five years old.

The now was changing me, and I could continue to let it change me for the worse, or I could switch course and change for the better.

I went from two hundred and twenty pounds to one-sixty-five through a solid year of good diet and exercise. I concentrated on making the change I wanted to happen. I walked everywhere. Through the snow of the Boston Garden, down Boylston Street and the South End. I was a walking machine. I gave myself a challenge to walk ten miles in a day every weekend. If you haven't been there, Boston is not exactly big, but I didn't let that stop me. Off I went, over the Longfellow Bridge into Cambridge, through Harvard Yard, stopping for coffee at the MIT campus, down the beautiful tree-lined Comm Ave, across the Boston Garden and Boston Common (I never quite grasped the difference), traipsing through the North End, dodging tourists, yuppies, and Italian grandmothers, before crashing at home, exhausted and proud.

I changed the now, even though it took work and facing the feelings behind my overeating.

Change is hard and scary, and we seem to expect some magical version of ourselves to arrive in a DeLorean to tell us what the future holds and show us what to do now that we have it all figured out. But that didn't work for Marty McFly, even with mad guitar skills. You can't wait for the perfect change to present itself, just like you can't wait for the perfect future to arrive. Sometimes you have to start walking when you only see a glimmer of hope.

In addiction circles, a common therapy is motivational interviewing that centers around Stages of Change, which provides a model for the big motivations that carry us through each stage of recovery, be it drugs, alcohol, binge eating, or other issues. One stage is called Contemplation. You know something's wrong but you aren't ready to do something about it. The next step is Action, as in you decide to do something about the wrongness. Beyond that is Maintenance, or said another way, Revision, because you may decide one day to quit cigarettes cold turkey but not succeed on the first try, hence you take a few bites at that particular apple.

You aren't going to hit the gym, lose a ton of weight, and never have to worry about regaining it. That's a fairy tale. My own weight has gone up and down several times after I first decided to get healthy. As of writing this book, I'm at a weight I'm not happy about. So what am I doing about it? I'm back with a personal trainer. I've put extra effort in on my elliptical machine at home. I'm cleaning out the junk food that's crept back into my diet. I'm making the changes I can to help myself.

When you get to Contemplation and recognize what you want to change, the Action of taking that first step towards something better doesn't have to be perfect. You don't know what the perfect steps are anyway. It's more important that you take any steps that are going in the general direction of the change you want to make.

Let's go back to the weight loss analogy. Where had I failed in my teens and twenties? I failed because I thought that running, swimming or bike riding was the answer to weight loss without also focusing on my diet or whether I even enjoyed those exercises or whether my body responded to them.

Over the years, I learned that my body hates running (my back having something to do with that). I'm just not built to be a runner. No matter how much I tried to force myself to run, thinking I'd get a positive outcome, that outcome never arrived. Was it good to get out the door and actually do something? Yes, there were times I lost weight. It just wasn't sustainable for me.

But it took those iterations of exercise to understand that running *doesn't* work for me. It took other iterations to understand weight lifting, walking, and biking were better. And ellipticals were better than those. It took a lot of small changes to figure out what would work to achieve the big change I wanted.

You can iterate on mistakes as well as successes. Finding out you don't like running is good to know and allows you to make the next change and do something else that you like better. The alternative is to wait for a perfect solution that somehow materializes out of thin air. But how would you know what solution would work without testing it? Without experimentation? Without experiencing it firsthand?

What if I had waited ten more years until I thought I had enough money for a personal trainer every day? Or to hire a dietician or chef that specializes in healthy eating? I would have been heavier and probably well into health complications.

THERE ARE NO PERFECT PATHS BUT MANY OKAY ONES.

You only know how something works after you've tried it out. I'm now in my early forties. What does that mean for me? It means some of the things I used to do aren't the things that I do now. I used to be able to lift more weight, go harder on my elliptical. Now I listen to my body, don't push it when it doesn't want it, focus on my diet more, and I walk more than ever.

Not only is every path an iterative journey, every *part* of the path is iterative. If I'd waited to do certain things in my life until my body was perfectly healthy, I'd still be waiting. The point is to get out the door, act, and figure out what works and what doesn't.

OUR JOB IS TO BE READY FOR THE PATH WHEN IT ANNOUNCES ITSELF.

This doesn't mean waiting forever for the perfect path to beat you over the head and present a wide flat road free of obstacles and clear signage of where to go next. What it means is you've noticed something needs to change and a small bright opening appears between the trees that could lead to this change.

Being curious about these small openings and insights and starting to move one foot in front of the other in the direction of those glimmers of light are the first steps toward change. Sometimes you're going to break out of the forest and just start running. Sometimes you'll be in the trees a long time taking baby steps through the brambles. But as long as you're thinking about taking that next step, you are moving. You're going down the right path—because the right path is any path that gets you out of the woods.

Revisiting Leia, she and her husband didn't need to wait until they had weeks of free time and a big budget to work with. They didn't need to do a yearlong tour of Europe on their first trip. They didn't need to wait for the perfect world traveler versions of themselves to arrive. There could have been small day or weekend excursions to local attractions. Then maybe a long holiday weekend to a resort in the next state over. Then a week in Mexico. They wanted to travel, the desire to change had announced itself, yet they put it off until not even a glimmer of light shone through the trees.

Change now or now will change you. You have to strike a balance between living practically and living adventurously. If you're waiting for something to change or happen in your life, there's never a better time than now to start making that change yourself.

No one gets out of life alive. We only have so much time, so many days, to take action. No matter how much money you have, or how much fame, or how much brain power, as of 2024 everyone dies. That day will arrive sooner or later, but it will arrive, so don't wait for a tomorrow you may not get.

CHAPTER 16

IF YOU PLAY DEAD TOO LONG, THE BEAR WILL EAT YOU ANYWAY

LANDO WAS A VERY PASSIVE GUY WHEN IT CAME TO MAKING changes in his life. He withdrew when confronted with challenges and obstacles. Lando's wife went into fight mode when she got activated. Lando, on the other hand, would always flee or freeze. Like a possum, he curled up and played dead. But each time he did this, the problems that triggered the attack never got addressed and he never repaired his connection to his wife. His passivity landed him in a deep cycle of avoidance. He knew it and let it take its course in whatever self-destructive way it would.

When change announces itself, for some, the instinct is to freeze and hope it will go away, as if change was a rampaging bear. I'm no bear expert; playing dead when a grizzly attacks is an old adage. But if you play dead after the bear has mozied on, it may come back. And be hungry. Or curious. A quick bite will satisfy both of those feelings for the bear, and playtime is suddenly over.

So why do we play dead too long? Why do we wait? Why are we so fearful of what comes next that we would rather stay in a Groundhog Day of unhappiness, endlessly repeating what doesn't work?

One word: fear. We're afraid that if we try something new and it doesn't work, then we will be in a worse place than where we started. News flash: that's going to happen sometimes in life. That's why life is iterative.

WE NEVER STAY IN ONE SPOT, GOOD OR BAD.

It's not about being stuck in a place that feels worse. It's about navigating your way out of the storms to something better. If your choice leads to a mistake, a feeling that you are further away from your goals, let that human-sized mess-up go and get on to the next thing. Outcomes don't have to be perfect, they just have to be different from the status quo.

Here's a thought experiment I use with clients, especially those thinking about stepping into the risky venture of entrepreneurship. Imagine you're on an island. The island may be small, the island may not have a lot of resources, but it's your island and you know it does the job. It's secure. But you want a better island. You don't think this island is going to fit your needs forever. And you look out over the horizon and across the sea and you're pretty sure there are more islands out there, but you really don't know. If you want a better island, at some point you have to take a guess as to where the next best one is, jump in the ocean, and swim in that direction.

It takes a major act of courage and faith to get into the water and just start swimming. There may be big waves, sharks, leg cramps—a whole host of risks without a guarantee you're going to find another island at all, let alone one that's bigger and better than the island you just left.

But what I see are people who jump into those uncharted waters and have a sense that there *is* a better island and they'll figure out how to get there even if they have to doggy-paddle. From experience, I can tell you the island they land on is almost always more fulfilling than their previous one.

So what happens to your life if you don't jump? What happens if you stay on your island and let the discomfort build until you realize all your resources are gone and you can no longer live in this place?

For those who stay on their too-small island, suddenly a storm blows in and the tides rise and the island they're on doesn't feel so safe and secure anymore. That's when I see people get dislodged, pushed out, and forced to swim away.

Rey, a multimillionaire who recently sold her company, finally came in and told me she was getting divorced. "I don't feel at home in my marriage anymore. I can't stop thinking about what my life would be like if I were single." The business had kept her in the marriage for a long time through financial entanglements with her husband. After it was sold, she realized those obstacles no longer existed. She thought thoughts she couldn't unthink as a new path opened up for her. The tides rose, the water came in, and she got dislodged from thinking she needed her marriage to fulfill an idea of the perfect life.

When we get stuck in a place we're not supposed to be, when we hang onto a person or job or identity that is detrimental to our self-concept and happiness, when we think the devil we know is more comfortable than the one we don't, eventually the storm of dysfunction we can't avoid makes us realize the status quo isn't working anymore.

The push off the island is usually subtle. It's the accumulation of small things, small thoughts that build up until one more, the last straw, causes you to jump because anything would be better than where you are now. Whatever misgivings or doubts you have about jumping pale in comparison to the discomfort that has now grown too big to ignore. That discomfort has been there a while but you just haven't noticed it, until, finally, you can't *not* notice it and the epiphany crystalizes that you have to change.

The slow build-up or realization that the island must be abandoned happens for the majority of people. But some people experience a sudden light-bulb moment that reveals everything.

When I was in college there was a famous goth bar nearby. Many years ago, a college friend from Germany, more into that scene than I was, found out I lived nearby and was beside herself. "My God, we have to go!" We got there and the bar was super dark. Synthy goth music pounded through the entire space. Everyone dripped in shiny black PVC, big black combat boots weighed down by dozens of buckles and lifted by three-inch soles, capes, corsets, and excessive amounts of metal accessories. You couldn't see anyone's real hair, as every head was covered in goggles, top hats, or hair falls made out of anything and everything: braided yarn, strips of leather, plastic tubing, every kind of black trim imaginable. And they were all dancing to the beat, on the small dance floor painted black, on the stage, and in giant birdcages stationed around the room. It was like being in an episode of HBO's sexy vampire series *True Blood*.

Then someone decided to smoke in the bathroom and set off the fire alarm. All the lights went on as the building was evacuated. Really on: harsh, fluorescent, glaring, and all at once. Suddenly, I saw the costumes were cheap, everyone was fifteen pounds heavier than they looked in the dark, and the bar was a disgusting expanse of old painted plywood. What was so cool and fascinating a moment before was totally different and much more real. I really hope they replaced that bar after all these years.

"The lights going on" are the thoughts and experiences that rapidly change your perspective. You can't unsee them. You can't unthink them. You can't hide from them anymore.

The possum defense may work for brief periods, but if you stay curled up in a ball too long, you'll starve or get dehydrated. You'll die anyway, with or without the bear.

If you play dead in life too long, life will eat you anyway.

Lando had prostate cancer a number of years ago. He's been in remission, but recently had some concerning results. He went through another round of radiation, but for a while he didn't know if he was going to make it. It put his life into perspective. "I don't want to fight with my wife anymore," he told me. "I don't know how much time I have left." Lando separated from his wife for a while and found a more peaceful way to live. He realized he didn't have to be the old version of himself. He didn't have to live on his too-small island.

At some point, we have to choose how we want our story to play out. Do we want to live in fear? In conflict? In stasis? Or do we want to take steps toward something more positive?

As humans, we take a lot of missteps. We experience a lot of pain. But as long as we're alive we can redefine our story. We can turn the page to another chapter with a different plot and character arc from the one we lived before.

The power to iterate, to let go, to be good enough, to connect, to change, all coalesce into the power of resilience. The ability to create, revise, repair the story of your life as long as you keep breathing.

PART 6

BUILDING RESILIENCE

CHAPTER 17

RESILIENCE ISN'T SHOWING UP WHEN IT'S ALL GREEN LIGHTS; IT'S SHOWING UP DESPITE A LOT OF RED ONES

IN 2022, I HEARD A TEDX TALK CALLED "THE GIFT AND Power of Emotional Courage" on resilience and experiencing uncomfortable emotions by Susan David. At one point, she summed up one of life's mysteries like this: "Tough emotions are part of our contract with Life." For me, that means something simple but profound. We will get sick. We will get hurt. We will die. These things will happen. It's just the "cost of admission," to borrow her phrase.

When we're in a place of hurt, in a place of "I don't know what comes next and I'm too afraid to take another step," it's a lot like drowning at night. It feels like you can't see what's going on; everything feels awful and terrible. You don't know which direction the shore lies. A big buoy clangs, one of those orange ones that guard harbors with a light and bell on top, and you have just enough strength to swim over to it and grab on. You cling to its sides for dear life, keeping your head above water. If there were light, you could see that the shortest route to shore is right over there, but fear and doubt keep you blinded in the dark, just surviving.

WHEN ALL HOPE FEELS LOST IN THE DARKNESS, YOU CLING TO WHATEVER YOU CAN.

You survive. But that's all you can do when clinging to a buoy in the ocean—survive. You're not living. You're not thriving. There is no way to improve your situation other than to start swimming toward the shore that you know is right there, even if you can't quite see it clearly through the morning light.

If we can't avoid the chaotic forces in life, if we indeed must accept life with all its imperfections and decay, then the only thing we can do is choose how we confront these things. Do we let them break us? Or do we bend around them?

In his book *The New Encyclopedia of Modern Bodybuilding*, Arnold Schwarzenegger speaks of getting a bad knee injury at the height of his bodybuilding days. He was competing in South Africa in 1971, when the stage collapsed and his knee was hurt pretty badly. One doctor told him rehabilitation would be long and tough and Schwarzenegger would be lucky to compete again even with surgery to repair it. So he found other doctors who weren't so pessimistic and were willing to help him toward his goal of doing competitive bodybuilding again. Sure enough, within a year or so, Schwarzenegger rehabbed the leg and avoided surgery. In the years that followed, he'd go on to win the Mr. Olympia title five times.

At the time of his accident, Schwarzenegger was probably one of the fittest people on the planet and even he couldn't prevent a random stage collapse from hurting him. All his strength and fitness didn't matter at that moment. His story of resilience wasn't about preventing the accident, or powering through it by himself; it was about how he took control of his recovery process and got the help he needed to get back on top. How he literally got back up.

Bad things are going to happen whether we want them to or not. Fast or slow. Big or small. We're going to get beaten up with time no matter how perfect we are or how much we prepare. No matter how wealthy or intelligent a person is, they can still die young of cancer. They can still end up in a plane crash. They can still burn themselves on a hot stove. There's no insulating yourself entirely from risk. Even a person who stays in bed all day long gets bedsores.

Problems and trauma don't have to occur dramatically all at once, like they did for Schwarzenegger. Sometimes our problems accumulate over time. "I didn't have any big childhood trauma," Arwen told me at our first meeting. Yet here she was, an alcoholic, with all sorts of other dysfunctions. "I always feel like my therapists are looking for the trauma," she continued, "but there's nothing I know of that would explain where all these problems came from."

YOU CAN SPLIT A BOULDER BY GIVING IT ONE MIGHTY WHACK, OR YOU CAN PUT IT IN THE MIDDLE OF A RIVER AND JUST GIVE IT TIME.

To explain this metaphor, think of a giant boulder that feels so steady and unbreakable—literally rock solid—and yet there are a couple ways to break it. You can hit it really hard with a sledgehammer, or you can put it in a river for a few thousand years. The water will eventually erode the boulder until it cracks, or until there's nothing left of it but pebbles. In the end, it is just as broken as it was with the sledgehammer. If resilience as it's understood in popular culture is never letting the sledgehammer hit you, I have news for you if you end up in the river.

There are a lot of ways to get hung up or blocked. What matters is what happens after that.

A lot of ink has been spilt by self-help gurus on resilience and the idea of fighting through getting knocked down or picking yourself back up. I admit I'm adding to this flood of ink. But resilience is also the acceptance that we're going to *get* knocked down, and it's *how* we get back up that matters, which is usually slow, messy, and with help. It's the lessons learned over a lifetime of being knocked over, pushed around, a little banged up, sometimes put back together. The strength is in what we learn, how it makes us grow, and in the act of getting back up.

There's a flip side to the Jeff Goldblum quote in *Jurassic Park*, "Life, uh, finds a way." Life finds a way to survive, as Goldblum's character, Ian Malcolm, means, but life also finds a way to kick your butt, which is maybe also a lesson in that movie as rampaging dinosaurs end up destroying a perfectly controlled human playground. After all, the humans spared no expense.

Eventually, we all get to an inflection point, a transition from one identity to another. Michael Phelps, for all his swimming prowess, couldn't keep winning Olympic gold medals forever. Now he's doing different things with his life that are equally valid. That's also resilience: not staying chained to a particular self-concept of who you were, even if that prior self was practically perfect at what it did.

Resilience isn't showing up when it's all green lights; it's showing up despite a lot of red ones. It's easy to keep fighting when everything is going your way and the path is open; it's much harder to keep going when you have a series of challenges or delays and curveballs you didn't account for. That's what resilience is: being able to still show up for yourself and others even after you get stopped. It's finding those alternate routes and taking the detour that will get you there, pivot as needed, not turning around and going home because you hit a red light.

When people stop and turn around, it's because they think they only get one try at this, and now that they've lost once, it is the final loss. There's no way back from here. They don't believe life is iterative, they think the first road is the only road. When life doesn't go the way they planned, when it gets scary, hard, insurmountable, they shut down. The physical injury becomes a moral injury to how things were supposed to go in their storybook life.

It's like the moment when the superhero encounters a villain stronger than they are who beats them, but instead of growing and finding another way to win, they pack up and leave. They wander in circles trying to find a path that was never there. That's preferable to getting back up to face that villain again, stricken with the fear they'll only get knocked down harder. And they would get knocked down again…if they don't let go of the old version of themselves and change.

Shedding an old superhero self that can no longer win is not giving up; it's letting go. Do you feel like old traumas or identities that keep you stuck are important to hold onto? Or is it time to open your hand and accept they've gotten you this far but are no longer a burden you need to carry?

Despite the encouragement of some popular self-help books, resilience from a therapeutic sense doesn't involve pushing yourself at all costs, up to and including the cost of your life. Resilience may fluctuate depending on the context. You'll have good times and bad.

WHEN CLIMBING MOUNT EVEREST, IT'S OKAY TO WAIT OUT THE STORM AT BASE CAMP.

There's no glory in freezing to death, or falling in a crevasse in a whiteout. Seasoned climbers know they'll get another chance at the summit.

Sometimes we just have to hunker down because we don't have the resources or abilities to confront an obstacle head-on. We aren't always in an okay place personally or mentally to move forward, and we have to be safely past immediate danger and threat before we can go from surviving to thriving. The trick is to not get stuck in base camp after the storm passes, and not be afraid to get back out there and try for the summit again.

Just as a river can wear you down slowly, building yourself back up can be just as slow.

Taking a pause for safe conditions to move, or repairing some storm damage, is not a weakness, because resilience isn't measured by how tough you are or how much pain you ignore. It's measured by how many times you can get back up. How many personal resources and supports you have that can help you rebuild and heal after each assault. How much damage you avoid or recover from because you were flexible enough to bend when you hit an obstacle, rather than break.

CHAPTER 18

RESILIENCE ISN'T MEASURED DAY TO DAY

WHEN WE EXERCISE HARD AND OUR MUSCLES CRAMP AND burn, that's the body losing oxygen and building up lactic acid in the muscles. Your body can't produce energy fast enough under extreme physical use to supply the muscles, so it switches to a mechanism that releases energy immediately but is incredibly inefficient and builds lactic acid, changing the pH, which cells don't like. Too much buildup means you have to stop and rest to recover.

What happens when you stop exercising? Well, all that acid gets taken into your liver, which reverses it all and puts you back to normal. But that reversal process can take at least twenty-four hours for most people, a whole day of recovery before you can engage in more strenuous exercise.

Dean Karnazes is a record-setting ultramarathon runner. He has an incredibly rare genetic condition, an "imperfection" in his

DNA, that allows his body to process lactic acid in real time. He can run fifty miles and not need a substantial break. A biological hiccup became Karnazes's greatest strength.

Accepting "imperfections" and learning how to either work with them or through them is another key component to building resilience. Vulnerabilities drive the cycle of create, revise, repair. If there's a crack in the marble, you're going to do your best to work it into the sculpture or work around it so as not to fracture the entire piece of art. You could try to reinforce it, cut it to put the weight distribution in such a way that the crack is held together by the weight of the stone rather than destroyed by it. Sometimes, like Brené Brown says, imperfections are gifts. I'd go a bit further and say imperfections are necessary as the building blocks of a resilient life. Not a life that's carved this time, but a life that's forged.

The secret to the katana of the ancient samurai is in its folds. Out of all metal swords made before the technological age, nothing matched the katana for strength and durability. To make a katana, two different steels have to be blended together. One is high-carbon, which is strong but brittle. The other is low-carbon, which is soft but malleable. The two steels, with their strengths and weaknesses, are fired and folded many times to create a blended steel, one that is both strong enough to hold a razor-sharp edge and flexible enough to absorb repeated impacts. So the secret of the sword's strength is not its hardness or ability to resist an immovable object—it's its flexibility. When the blade encounters an immovable object, it curves around or bends away from it. Pure metal doesn't work that way. Its singular molecular structure makes it strong in only one way. If pressure is applied in any other way, the metal fails.

Unlike a soft sword that bends, a hard sword shatters under pressure.

This is similar to how bones work. To hold up to the multiple kinds of stresses encountered in day-to-day physical activity, bones need to have a mix of calcium, for hardness, and collagen, for flexibility. People born without enough collagen experience osteogenesis imperfecta, or brittle bone disease. Literally meaning "imperfect bone growth." Every small bump or fall, even just picking up a box, can cause their bones to fracture, and it takes longer for the bones to heal.

A katana has to be remade ten to twenty times before the blade can withstand the stresses of battle and time. Each time it comes out of the fire, it is hammered anew, the steel folded to make the sword stronger than the last iteration. For a katana, the resilience of any given moment is counted in small folds, the new one added to those that came before.

YOU ARE THE SWORD BEING FOLDED. IT'S JUST A QUESTION OF WHICH FOLD YOU'RE ON.

Resilience isn't something you do quickly, or all at once. It's built a little at a time, step by step, layer by layer, fold by fold. The ability to think iteratively, that an outcome is just one version of several, contributes to our overall resilience.

There are going to be a lot of times when, despite your best efforts, life knocks you down. That's a given. But it's not getting knocked down that determines who we are in life, it's how we get back up. As the old Japanese proverb goes, "Nana karobi, ya oki"—fall down seven times, stand up eight.

LIFE ISN'T SOMETHING YOU WIN OR LOSE.

Life is going to kick your butt. It's going to hurt. It's going to suck sometimes. But your ability to be resilient isn't measured on any given day when life's kicking your ass. It's measured on all the others.

CHAPTER 19

BECOMING UNBREAKABLE

WHEN I WAS FIVE YEARS OLD, I WATCHED THE MOVIE *Jaws*. It was being featured on one of the classic movie channels on TV. Afterward, I was convinced that Jaws could get into our swimming pool. I was so convinced I kept turning around to look when I was underwater.

One bad story, and suddenly there are sharks everywhere. Every time you get in the water, you hear *duh duh, duh duh, duda duda duda*. Eventually, even kiddie pools look dangerous.

When I met Galadriel, she was going through a terrible divorce. She had a lot of trauma associated with it that resulted in debilitating grief and PTSD. We talked about how she got triggered during the divorce proceedings. She was already in a dark place because of the events that led up to the divorce and didn't have a lot of reserves left to handle the demands of her life falling apart legally and publicly. So every time she had to do even a little thing like review a document, she'd get panic attacks. Her story reminded me of the time when I was underwater, looking for sharks everywhere.

But the problem with being underwater and in a panic for a while, is that even after you've got your head above water, something as small as rain starts to feel like you're drowning again. This is when you know you have little to no resilience left, at least for that type of situation.

Resilience at its simplest is stress tolerance. It's the ability, despite any previous experience with being underwater, to recognize and accept the next storm as just rain, and not something that will necessarily pull you under. When a new stress test occurs, a new challenge or obstacle or hard stretch of life, if you have a buildup of resilience, you may swallow a few mouthfuls of water, you may be cold and wet, but you won't panic and drown. You'll be able to swim through this next storm.

We're often oblivious to the level of resilience we possess until it is tested. I remember an old interview, the source now lost to the ebb and flow of time and the internet, that told how Scarlett Johansson got into phenomenal shape for her role of Black Widow in the Marvel movies. Months into her regimen she had her doubts about how well she was doing building up her superhero body.

"Do I suck at this?" she asked her trainer. "Why is this still so hard?"

"No, you don't suck," he responded. "I've been making it harder as you get stronger. You just didn't see your progress along the way."

As we get stronger, we can take on more challenges. Our resilience increases with exercise and practice. Life will take on more complexity as you grow better able to handle more complexity. You can make things harder, or easier, depending on your level of resilience at that time and place. That is proof that you are more resilient. You can handle more.

Your brand of resilience determines how you weather your rivers and your tidal waves. How do you put yourself back together after the boulder's been cracked? Do you use a quick-drying but weak glue? Do you let the pieces stay shattered? Or do you use seams of strong gold alloy, like those Japanese kintsugi vases mentioned earlier, that look all the more beautiful for their meticulously repaired fractures?

Is a vase resilient for never having been broken, or is it resilient for becoming something new that's stronger and more beautiful than before?

Resilience isn't measured day-to-day. It's measured by the number of times you're put in the fire, and how many folds you forge from that pain.

It's measured by your ability to iterate, to take the opportunities and chances that come.

It's measured by your ability to let go of perfection.

It's measured by feeling you are good enough to let good things happen to you and for you.

It's measured by the intimate connections you make.

And it's measured by choosing change, even when you don't feel you're ready.

Resilience isn't measured in a moment; it's built up over a lifetime of challenge and hardship. It's not hardening yourself into an immovable object. Immovable objects don't exist in real life. And since life is iterative and moves all the time, the more immovable you become, the more life will just pass you by, wearing you down like a boulder in a river.

So what happens when an immovable object encounters an unstoppable force?

In the early days of the solar system, when the earth was still a molten ball of rock, a rather large object crashed into it. Scientists speculate that this now extinct celestial body could have been a giant asteroid, or maybe another infant planet competing for the same orbit as earth. Whatever the case, the impact was immense, almost destroying the earth before it ever got started. As it was, a quarter of earth's mass was expelled into space, got caught in earth's gravity, and took up an orbit around the shocked planet that had literally pulled itself back together. This large chunk of expelled rock formed a sphere and became the Moon.

Why is that important? Because one of the leading theories for the earth's unusual environmental stability compared to its neighboring rocky planets is because of the moon and its influence on the development of liquid water, tides, and weather patterns. Life may have been very different, or nonexistent, if it wasn't for the moon.

So a catastrophic event, so terrible in its act, created an environment necessary for life. What's more, if the earth hadn't been molten and flowing, giving to the pressure, an impact that size would have destroyed it.

The earth always seems like it has existed forever, but even it was broken at some point. Yet it survived because it flowed around a pressure point, absorbed it, and became something new with the help of its broken pieces.

And that's the trick of this thought experiment. No object is immovable, and no force is unstoppable. Those ideas violate the laws of physics.

Now, finally, I can let you in on the secret of life.

NOTHING IS REALLY UNBREAKABLE.

Doing life right is not about becoming a perfect unbreakable version of yourself, or choosing the path with no obstacles or pain. Those things don't exist.

How you become unbreakable is to accept that you do, in fact, break. That you are made up of strong stuff *and also* imperfections and cracks earned through a lifetime of getting hit and getting back up. And that these imperfections and cracks are just a part of life and, most importantly, *can be repaired.*

So, in essence, a resilient, unbreakable you is a you that believes, deep down, that everything can be fixed. Not to the way it was before, but to a different version of you, an evolved version, one that can move forward into the next chapter of life. One that is happy to keep living.

I'd love to end on a positive note with an update on the stories of some of the clients who appear above, but the reality is that there is no period at the end of their stories. Whether with me or with others, their stories go on. But the fact that those stories are still being written, that they've come in seeking help and a better way forward, *is* the story of resilience. Because real resilience doesn't end with a period either. Resilience is a by-product of experience—the taking of chances. It's a repeated cycle of create, revise, and repair. As long as we keep working through that cycle and maintain the desire and ability to adapt and get better, we are still adding folds to our lives and building the resilience that will make getting back up easier.

The mental and emotional work outlined in this book is the key to building resilience, and resilience is the key to becoming a happier you. An "unbreakable" you. Not because you'll never be worn or chipped or broken—that's just part of life—but because you'll know you can always put yourself back together again, and that new iteration of you will be better than the one before.

The key to becoming an unbreakable you is to never stop becoming.

We can't be unbreakable. But we can create. We can revise. We can repair. As long as we keep to this cycle of constantly iterating on ourselves, constantly maintaining and adding to our skills and connections and identities, we'll bend. We'll flex. We'll find a way, no matter what life throws at us.

We'll not only survive but thrive.

CONCLUSION

THE SECRET TO CHOOSING THE RIGHT PATH IS THIS: THERE is no right path. There never was. The right path, just like Neo's digital spoon or Magritte's painting of a pipe, is a human metaphor. An idea of a life, not the life itself. It only has the meaning we give it after looking back on the choices and experiences that made it. And no matter how far down the path you look to see where it might lead, you can't anticipate what shows up beyond the next bend.

You don't have to be a certain way to travel a certain path. Certainty is the antithesis of life. And it won't get you to your goals, no matter how many times you've been told it will. And pounding yourself against the unmovable wall that is the ideal or the expected only brings more pain and immobility.

Life is an iterative process and best done through experience. You'll get far more chances than you think you're going to make a go of it; you just have to be able to believe you're good enough to take them.

Let go of notions of "good" and "bad." Reject the need to choose the "right way" versus any way. A wonderful life is done in shades of gray, not black and white. There is no correct instruction manual for how to live your life, and in the end, you are the driver and the determiner of your direction, and it's your opinion of that direction that matters. So let go of who you think you *should* be, and embrace who you think you *could* be.

"Am I good enough?" is the wrong question to ask. You *are* good enough to take the next steps. There is no perfect story of you. No right way to do life. You're not the sum of your mistakes, and though mistakes can hurt you, they don't have to break you.

Relationships create the life preserver that will keep you afloat. Make connections along the way to reinforce the good things about you, and accept that you are good enough to have connections. Everyone wants to be loved and accepted by those we choose to love and accept. Find the people who can share your vulnerabilities and make you feel good about being you.

Make a change every day. Making change gets easier the more you do it. Don't be afraid to take a path because it isn't perfect. You can't wait for tomorrow to take chances. If you wait too long, you're going to find yourself at the end of your life never having lived it.

Resilient people are not pure iron; they are a blend of alloys that have been fired many times, folded over, hammered together into a seamless whole that bends when struck instead of breaking. Everything we do to be more flexible and adaptable makes us stronger and more resilient to future change and obstacles.

The secret to an unbreakable you is not becoming unbreakable, it's becoming infinitely creative. Revisable. Repairable. It's the ability to come up against hardship, learn from the experience, pick up the pieces, and go back to the forge to remake yourself.

Create, revise, repair is a constant cycle. You're going to have cracks in the marble. You're going to get dislodged from the island. Something will get worn down, illness will happen, accidents will stop you in your tracks. You can't prevent any of that from happening.

But you can choose how you will move with and through those challenges.

If you're holding yourself to a standard that no one else is asking of you, and there are parts of your life that make you afraid to move in a different direction, the next step forward is to seek out the support from professional mental health providers who can help you walk out of those woods. They'll be able to assess your strengths and see when you need to rest and when you can sprint forward. That's their job, to help clarify which steps you want to take through your life transitions, and how to make those steps manageable. Just by reading this book, you're seeing the light between the trees.

So step toward it. One foot at a time.

ACKNOWLEDGMENTS

THANK YOU TO MY FRIENDS, FAMILY, AND LOVED ONES, WHO have carried me when I needed it, been there when I doubted anyone should, and have hung in there long enough to know I love them and couldn't have done it without them. Thank you to my many mentors for teaching me right from wrong on numerous levels.

And thank you, Quint. You're a good boy.

ABOUT THE AUTHOR

JON DEAM, MD, is a board-certified psychiatrist, addiction specialist, and founder of Aveo Wellness, a concierge psychiatry and wellness practice. Find out more about Aveo Wellness at www.AveoWell.com.

Dr. Jon has worn many hats, from training in an inner-city Boston hospital, being the head doctor at a few psychiatric hospitals across the United States, to now working with entrepreneurs, C-suite executives, and celebrities to help them achieve their dreams by shaking off old perceptions and stepping into new life chapters.

Media appearances include *The D Spot* with Dr. Dana McNeil and *Diving into Healing*.

He lives in San Diego, California, where he practices psychiatric medicine, in addition to Los Angeles and New York. He is a lover of music and a player of many, many guitars.

www.ingramcontent.com/pod-product-compliance
Lightning Source LLC
Chambersburg PA
CBHW060529080526
44586CB00012B/672